How to Play Electric Guitar

Easy-to-Read • Easy-to-Play
Effects, Styles & Technique

Tony Skinner, Alan Brown
& Jake Jackson

FLAME TREE
PUBLISHING

Publisher and Creative Director: Nick Wells
Project Editor: Polly Prior
Consultant: Jake Jackson
New Photography: Stephen Feather
Art Director: Mike Spender
Layout Design: Jake

21
5 7 9 10 8 6 4

This edition first published 2011 by
FLAME TREE PUBLISHING
6 Melbray Mews
Fulham, London SW6 3NS
United Kingdom
www.flametreepublishing.com

Music site: www.flametreemusic.com

ISBN 978-1-84786-716-2

A CIP record for this book is available from the
British Library upon request.

Acknowledgements
All photographs, diagrams and notation courtesy of Foundry Arts.

Printed in China

Contents

Introduction

If music is a universal language, there is no instrument more global than the guitar. It is easy to see why. It's a great do-it-yourself invention: like the piano, on a guitar it's relatively easy to play a melody and rhythm simultaneously but, unlike a piano, a guitar is portable.

In recent times, the guitar has always been at the forefront of music. It played a key role in the birth of rock'n'roll, and continues to defy predictions of its impending demise brought on by the innovations of synthesizer technology and computer-driven music. The allure of the guitar also lies in the fact that it is a popular beginner instrument. Even if you have only been playing for a short while, the rewards can be great. And it is worth sticking with it. In the 50 years since it began to replace the piano as the most popular instrument with beginner musicians, the guitar is still providing new sounds, new tones and new avenues for expression.

The rewards for a guitar player are great, and this book will provide any beginner with a solid grounding in the fundamentals and with more advanced techniques. It covers the basics of guitar playing – how to strum, pick and create simple note sequences. You'll find out how to use timing, how to read chord charts and understand keys, musical notation and essential harmonic tools, like chords, notes and scales. You'll master vibrato and string bends, and when you are ready, you will move on to arpeggios and other more advanced techniques. You will also learn how to alter your sound using some of the most common effects, and how to take care of your electric guitar. And we will give you a taster of the heights you could achieve by including a specially selected variety of tunes in the style of various well-known guitar heroes.

Once you have got to grips with the basics, keep going and practise, practise, practise. The journey of a thousand miles begins with a single chord, or riff, or lick. Turn the page, and enjoy the journey.

Authors

Tony Skinner (text) is widely respected as one of the UK's premier music educators. He is the director of the Registry of Guitar Tutors – the world's foremost organization for guitar education. He is also the principal guitar examiner for London College of Music Exams and has compiled examination syllabi in electric, bass and classical guitar playing, as well as popular music theory, rock/pop band and popular music vocals. He has written and edited over 50 music-education books, and is the editor of *Guitar Tutor* magazine and a columnist for *Total Guitar* magazine.

Alan Brown (new musical examples) is a former member of the Scottish National Orchestra. He now works as a freelance musician, with several leading UK orchestras, and as a consultant in music and IT. Alan has had several compositions published, developed a set of music theory CD-Roms, co-written a series of Bass Guitar Examination Handbooks and worked on over 100 further titles.

Jake Jackson (consultant) is a musician and songwriter with a number of music instruction titles to his credit, including *Guitar Chords, Piano Chords, Learn to Play Flamenco* and *Scales & Modes.*

1

2

3

4

5

6

7

8

9

10

11

12

Before You Begin

Before you learn how to play the electric guitar, it's important to know a little about the instrument itself. What are its origins? How does it differ from its acoustic cousin? How does it work? It's also vital to know how to tune your instrument and how to warm up properly. Then you can get down to the real business of learning how to play it.

1
2
3
4
5
6
7
8
9
10
11
12

The Electric Guitar

The electric guitar is a marriage of twentieth-century technology with the time-honoured convenience and playability of the classical and Spanish guitar. The first electric versions of the acoustic guitar were made in the early 1900s, a result of ongoing efforts by inventors, tinkerers and musicians. In the 1950s, Leo Fender developed the first mass-produced and affordable electric guitar.

First Electric Guitars

Some of the earliest electric guitars adapted hollow-bodied acoustic instruments and used tungsten pickups. This type of guitar was first manufactured in 1931 by the Electro String

A Fender Telecaster, one of the most successful electric guitars.

Instrument Corporation under the direction of Adolph Rickenbacher and George Beauchamp. The guitar was called a 'Rickenbacker'. Another early solid-body electric guitar was designed and built by musician and inventor Les Paul in the early 1940s. His 'log guitar' consisted of a 4 x 4 wood post with a neck attached to it and home-made pickups and hardware.

In 1946, Leo Fender designed the first commercially successful solid-body electric guitar with a single magnetic pickup, initially named the 'Esquire'. The two-pickup version of the Esquire was called the 'Broadcaster', later becoming known as the 'Telecaster'.

The Gibson Les Paul, with the famous starburst look.

1

How Do They Work?

Electric guitars make sound by creating electro-magnetic induction through pickups containing a few thousand turns of fine enamelled copper wire wrapped around a permanent magnet. The single-coil pickup can have subtle variances in tone, even when mass-produced successfully, as were the classic pickups of the original Telecaster and Stratocaster. That's why some Strats may sound magnificent and others merely acceptable. One problem with single-coil electro-magnetic pickups is that they pick up hum along with the musical signal.

Single-coil pickups on a Fender Stratocaster. These are used to detect the vibrations of a guitar string that can then be amplified.

The desire to be rid of this unwanted hum resulted in the humbucking pickup, which comprises two standard pickups wired together with identical coils bathed in fields of opposite magnetic polarity. The two coils are wired to cancel the hum produced by each. The signal from the vibrations of the guitar strings is captured by both pickups and added together, doubling the output. Side effects are a rounder tone with fewer highs than that produced by a Strat or Tele, and a hotter signal more easily able to overdrive an amp for a warm distortion effect.

A super humbucker V2 pickup on an Ibanez Studio electric guitar. Humbucking pickups are generally made up of two single pickups wired together.

15

1
2
3
4
5
6
7
8
9
10
11
12

1

2

3

4

5

6

7

8

9

10

11

12

Anatomy of an Electric Guitar

The electric guitar is not complex, but the pieces of the electric guitar must fit together and match each other perfectly.

Here are some of the most important ingredients.

❶ The Fingerboard

This covers the face of the neck and provides a playing surface for the guitarist. Frets are set into the fingerboard enabling the guitarist to find and stop the string at the desired point. Fingerboards are generally made of maple or rosewood, although some manufacturers are now making fingerboards from synthetic materials such as graphite.

❷ The Body

This is usually wooden: ash, elder or basswood. Expensive US-produced guitars are made of rare

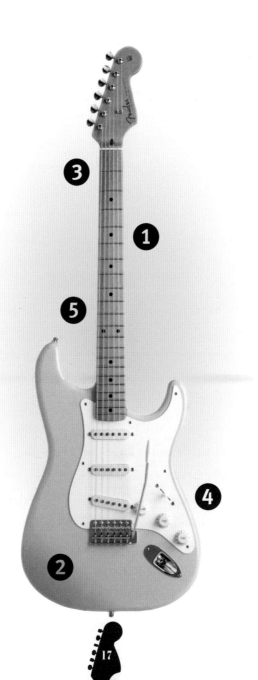

1
2
3
4
5
6
7
8
9
10
11
12

hardwoods such as mahogany and maple. As good-quality wood becomes harder to obtain, guitars are nearly always made of one or more pieces of wood sandwiched together. Ibanez has created guitars with no wooden parts, while Gibson's 'Smart Wood' range are made from wood cut from sustainable forests.

❸ Nut and Frets

The nut is placed at the end of the fingerboard just below the headstock, where it provides one of the two anchor points (the other being the bridge saddle at the other end of the guitar) for the string. Nickel silver frets are fitted to the fingerboard underneath the strings. The frets are placed at precise points on the fingerboard to enable the guitarist to play in tune. Frets wear down over time and change the tone of the guitar. The distance between the nut and the bridge saddle is important and dictates the scale of the guitar. Fender instruments have a 63.5-cm (25-in) scale while Gibson instruments have a 61-cm (24-in) scale.

❹ Hardware

Pickups, bridge and electronics are fundamental to the tone of the electric guitar. Single-coil pickups produce a bright sound; twin-coil pickups have a warmer, less defined sound. Bridges are usually adjustable, which lets you adjust the action (height) of the strings and helps keep the guitar's intonation true. Bridge assemblies may be either fixed or vibrato (tremolo) models. Certain guitars also have a hardware tailpiece, in which the strings terminate, rather than a string-through design, in which strings are fed through the back of the guitar, over the bridge and stretched to the tuners on the headstock.

❺ The Neck

The neck is often made from dense maple or ash. The wood needs to be stable as the neck is under tension. If the neck is screwed to the body it is called a 'bolt-on neck'. Necks that are jointed to the body are called 'set-in'. Bolted and jointed necks have different tonal characteristics: bolted necks are thought to be brighter, while set-in neck guitars have a rounded tone.

1

2

3

4

5

6

7

8

9

10

11

12

Amplification

When it comes to playing electric guitar, the
amplifier is an extension of the instrument itself.

How Do They Work?

In order for the relatively low electrical output
generated by the coils of the pickup to drive the cone
of a speaker, the current must be increased – or
'amplified'. A guitar amplifier takes power from an
external electrical source (outlet or battery) and
controls the delivery of that power to the speaker
according to the level of the voltage from the pickups.
This can be accomplished by using valves (tubes),
solid-state chips or a combination of both.

The Vox AC30 is the
amplifier that will
forever be linked with
the Beatles and the
British Invasion of
the 1960s.

The first amplifiers were of relatively low wattage (10–20 watts), while some of the early pickups were quite powerful, easily capable of driving those fledgling combos into a mild distortion. It was only later, as the amps got more powerful, and some of the single-coil pickups less so, that you began to hear cleaner tones.

New Amp Technology

For over half a century, the guitar amplifier remained virtually unchanged. Only with the advent of cheap DSP (digital signal processing) chips have we started to see some new twists on the old formula. Multiple onboard effects and amp modelling have become possible, but certain things still remain the same: for the most part, more volume requires a bigger amplifier. The trend towards more power in smaller cheaper packages that has swept through most technologies has not quite overtaken the art of guitar amplification. In the quest for guitar tone, bigger still produces louder, and better usually means more expensive.

Which Amp To Buy?

Different styles of music require different amplifiers. Country, jazz and funk need clean tones, often at high volume; an amplifier with plenty of 'headroom' (60–100 watts), such as Fender's Twin Reverb, works best. Rock or pop rock requires good crunch tones; try the Fender Super Reverb, Vox AC30 and the Marshall 50-watt heads or combos. For metal, you want high output and edgy distortion, so consider Marshall 100-watt stacks, Mesa Boogie Rectifiers or Peavey Triple XXX models.

Remember Your Guitar

When shopping for an amplifier, be sure to bring the main guitar that you will be playing. You don't want to judge it with a guitar that doesn't sound like yours. If there is a return policy, try to play it in your rehearsal space. If not, try to go to the shop early on a weekday – at a quiet shopping time they might let you crank up the volume a little.

Say No To Gimmicks

Remember that great basic tone is far more important than bells and whistles. You can always add distortion and other outboard effects later, but if the amplifier's unadorned sound doesn't do it for you, no amount of add-ons will make it better. Finally, trust your ears; if you think that it sounds good, it does sound good. There is no arbiter of tone. This is part of your musical voice and should reflect your particular taste, not some consensus.

There's no need to spend a fortune – a Tone King Imperial (left), Fender Blues Junior (middle) or Fender Hot Rod Deluxe (right) won't break the bank, but will give you a terrific tone.

Tuning

Tuning is the first skill any guitarist has to master: no matter how well you play, it won't sound any good if the guitar is out of tune.

Pitch

A guitar can be tuned so that all the strings are 'in tune' with one another, and this can sound fine if you are playing alone or unaccompanied. However, if you intend to play with other musicians or along to a recording, then you'll need to make sure that your guitar is tuned to 'concert pitch'. Technically, that means that the note

Tuners come in many different shapes and sizes – mobile phone apps (such as those for use on the Apple iPhone) are increasingly popular and easy to use.

A, when played on the fifth fret of the first string (the A above middle C on a piano), is vibrating at 440 hertz (cycles per second). In practice, guitarists in a band will usually tune up to a keyboard or use an electronic tuner for reference. Acoustic guitarists sometime still use a tuning fork to find a 'true' pitch.

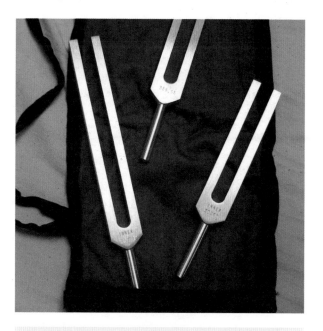

A tuning fork is normally used to find the 'true' pitch and is easy to carry in a bag.

Tuning at the Fifth Fret

The open strings of the guitar, from the lowest note
(thickest string) to the highest (thinnest string),
should be tuned as follows.

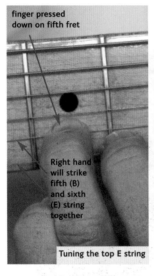

finger pressed
down on fifth fret

Right hand
will strike
fifth (B)
and sixth
(E) string
together

Tuning the top E string

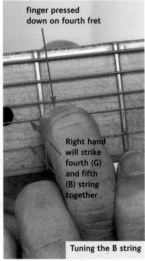

finger pressed
down on fourth fret

Right hand
will strike
fourth (G)
and fifth
(B) string
together

Tuning the B string

Once you have tuned the low string to the pitch of
E you can use this as the starting point from which
to tune all the other strings.

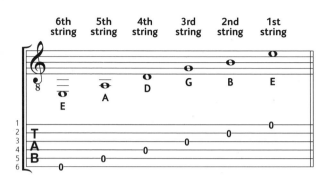

1. Begin by playing a note on the fifth fret of the low E string; this will produce the note A. You should then turn the fifth string machine head (tuning peg) until the pitch of this open string matches the fretted note on the lower string. If the open fifth string sounds higher than the fretted A note then you should rotate the machine head to slacken the string; if open fifth string sounds too low then you should tighten the string.

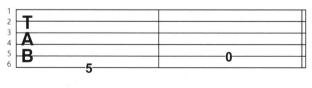

A on the 6th string   **Open A string**

2. Once you have tuned the A string, you can produce the note of D by picking a note at the fifth fret; this will provide you with the pitch you need to tune the open D string accurately. You can then use the same method for tuning the open G string, i.e. by adjusting it to match the note played on the fifth fret of the D string.

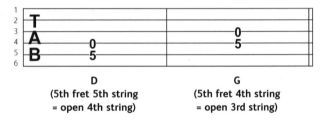

D
(5th fret 5th string
= open 4th string)

G
(5th fret 4th string
= open 3rd string)

3. The procedure changes slightly when you come to the B string. You need to tune this to the pitch of the note on the fourth fret of the G string. Once the B string is in tune, fretting it at the fifth fret will produce the note E; you should adjust the open first string to match this pitch.

B
(4th fret 3rd string
= open 2nd string)

E
(5th fret 2nd string
= open 1st string)

Once you've completed this process, listen closely to various chords at different positions on the neck and make any final tuning adjustments.

It's important to remember that a guitar is not a synthesizer, and characteristic imperfections in a guitar's components can affect its intonation (the accuracy of its pitch at all positions) as well as its tone. These characteristics are not necessarily bad things and can give a guitar a unique personality. They can also make it easier or harder to keep a guitar in tune.

1

2

3

4

5

6

7

8

9

10

11

12

Tip

Unless you are fitting new strings,
you will not need to make large turns on
the machine heads. If you tune your guitar
regularly, then a few small tuning adjustments
should be all it normally needs.

You should now be able to have a go at tuning your guitar.

Warming Up

Music may come from the head and heart, but your body gives the physical delivery – and that is why guitarists should be prepared. Just as with athletes, the best results will come when you have woken up the relevant muscles, rather than starting from cold.

Stretching your wrists, hands and fingers is a good starting point, and should precede any actual playing. Pressing palm to palm and bending each hand in turn to make a 90-degree angle – a little beyond, if possible – can be followed by bending back individual fingers. Repeat the process three or four times, then try pairs of fingers.

Exercise can help you avoid tendonitis, carpal tunnel syndrome and other repetitive stress injuries. But they can also help you play better and achieve greater speed. So take care of yourself – no one else will!

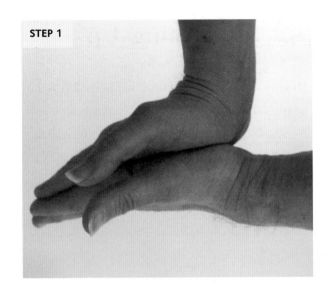

STEP 1

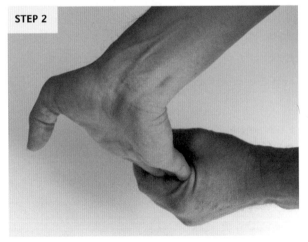

STEP 2

STEP 3

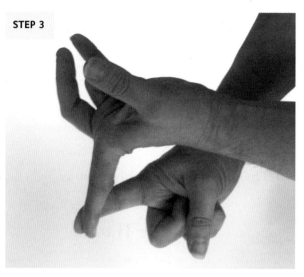

STEP 4

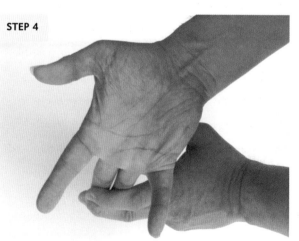

1

2

3

4

5

6

7

8

9

10

11

12

Hand Positions

If you don't position your hands in the optimum way, learning to play guitar might prove to be an uphill struggle; playing with a good technique from the start, by positioning your hands correctly, will make learning new techniques relatively easy.

Fretting Hand

1. Regardless of whether you are playing chords or single notes, you should always press the fretting-hand fingers as close to the fretwire as possible. This technique minimizes the unpleasant 'fretbuzz' sounds that can otherwise occur. Pressing at the edge of the fret also greatly reduces the amount of pressure that is required, enabling you to play with a lighter and hence more fluent touch.

The optimum position for your hand when you are fretting a note: fingers are close to the frets, which minimizes any fretbuzz.

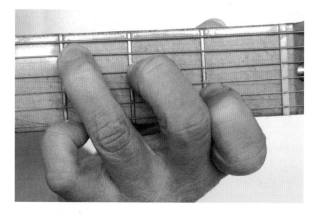

2. Try to keep all the fretting-hand fingers close to the fingerboard so that they are hovering just above the strings ready to jump into action. This minimizes the amount of movement required when moving from one chord or note to another. To do this, your thumb should be placed at the centre of the back of the guitar neck, your fingers arching over the fretboard to descend more or less vertically on the strings.

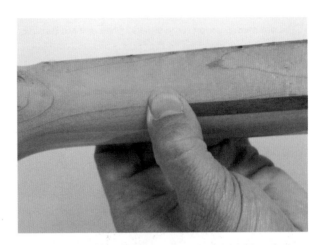

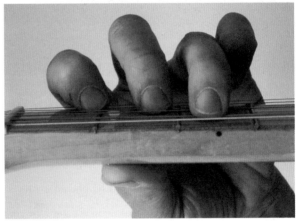

Correct hand position – your thumb should be placed
at the centre of the back of the guitar neck, your fingers
arching over the fretboard to descend more or less
vertically on the strings.

36

3. Unless you are playing more than one note with the same finger, you should always use the tips of your fingers to fret notes; this will produce the sound more directly and cleanly than using the fleshier pads of the fingers.

Picking Hand

1. If you're using a plectrum (pick), grip it between the index (first) finger and the thumb. Position the plectrum so that its tip extends only just beyond the fingertip, by about $\frac{1}{10}$ in (2.5 mm). Whilst this measurement doesn't have to be exact, make sure that the amount of plectrum that extends beyond the index finger is not excessive: this would result in a lack of pick control, making the plectrum liable to flap around when striking the strings – reducing both fluency and accuracy. Alternatively, if you find that when you try to pick a string you often miss it completely, the cause is most likely to be not enough plectrum extending beyond the fingertip.

1

2. Although you need to hold the plectrum with a small amount of pressure so that it doesn't get knocked out of your hand when you strike the strings, be very careful not to grip the plectrum too tightly. Excessive gripping pressure can lead to muscular tension in the hand and arm, with a subsequent loss of flexibility and movement.

3. The most efficient way to pick single notes is to alternate between downstrokes and upstrokes.

Avoid holding the plectrum at right angles to your index finger, otherwise your wrist may lock.

Unless you want to achieve a particular staccato sound, this 'alternate picking' technique should be used for all melodies or lead-guitar playing. (For information on finger-picking, see pages 58-62.)

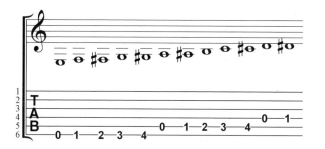

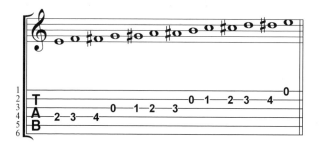

The E chromatic scale consists of a continual series of half steps, which means that every note in 'open position' is played. This makes the scale ideal for building technique as it uses all four fingers to fret notes. It should be played using alternate down and up plectrum strokes.

39

1
2
3
4
5
6
7
8
9
10
11
12

2

Quick Start

This is where you start learning the
techniques that you will always rely on
as an electric guitar player – strumming
and picking. You'll also discover an
essential part of every player's
vocabulary: chords. Finally, you will
take a look at major and minor keys.

First Chords

Chords form the backbone of all music. As soon as you've mastered a few chord shapes you'll be well on the road to music-making. The really great thing about chords is that once you've learnt them they'll last you a lifetime: you'll still be using any chord you learn today 20 years from now.

Chord Symbols

There are two main types of chords that form the core of most popular music: 'major chords' and 'minor chords'.

1. The chord symbol that tells you when to play a major chord is simply the letter name of the chord written as a capital. For example, the chord symbol for the G major chord is 'G' and the chord symbol for the D major chord is 'D'. Major chords have a bright, strong sound.

2. Minor chord symbols consist of the capital letter
of the chord name followed by a lowercase 'm'. For
example, the chord symbol for the E minor chord is
'Em' and the chord symbol for the A minor chord is
'Am'. Minor chords have a mellow, sombre sound.

Chord Name	Chord Symbol
C major	C
C minor	Cm
D major	D
D minor	Dm
E major	E
E minor	Em
F major	F
F minor	Fm
G major	G
G minor	Gm
A major	A
A minor	Am
B major	B
B minor	Bm

Fretboxes

Guitar chord fingerings are written in diagrams known as 'fretboxes'. These indicate the strings and frets that are used for the chord, and which fingers should be used for fretting the notes.

An X above a string line means this string should not be played.

An 0 above a string line means this string should be played open (unfretted).

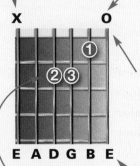

The thick line at the top of the fretbox represents the nut of the guitar, and the remaining horizontal lines represent the frets.

The recommended fret-hand fingering is shown in simple numbered circles:

❶ = index finger
❷ = middle finger
❸ = third finger
❹ = little finger

Fretboxes are written with vertical lines representing the strings: the low E string is represented by the line on the far left and the high E string by the line on the far right.

Starting Chords

Using the next few pages, begin with E minor, as this involves only two fretted notes and uses plenty of open strings. Place your fingers on the strings, pressing lightly yet securely with the fingertips, and then strum across all six strings. Once you're familiar with this chord, move your two fretting fingers from E minor on to the adjacent higher strings, and add the first finger on the first fret of the B string – this is A minor. Notice that the low E string should be omitted when you strum A minor.

Next try some major chords. If G major seems like too much of a stretch between the second and third fingers, allow your thumb to move down to the centre of the back of the guitar neck until the chord feels comfortable. Notice that only the top four strings should be strummed when playing D major.

Em

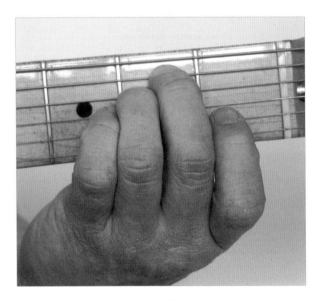

46

Am

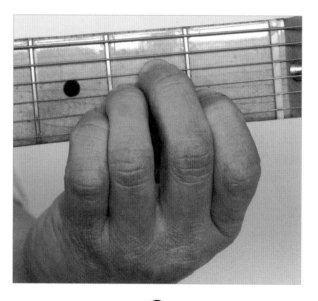

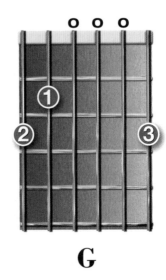

G

X X O

D

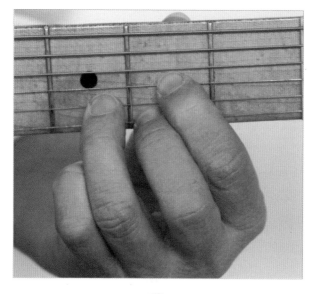

1 2 3 4 5 6 7 8 9 10 11 12

49

Simple Chord Sequences

Many songs consist of a short chord sequence that is repeated throughout. Once you have learnt a couple of basic chord shapes you can start playing a chord sequence by changing from one chord to another. It's then only a short step before you can play the chords to a complete song.

Minor Chords

Begin by strumming downwards four times on an E minor chord, then without stopping change to A minor and play another four strums, keeping the same tempo. Without stopping or hesitating, move your fingers back to E minor and continue strumming so that the whole sequence begins again.

Notice the similarity of the E minor and A minor chord shapes: the second and third fingers are used at the second fret in both chords, the only difference being that they move from the A and D strings in E minor to the adjacent D and G strings in A minor. Try to keep this in mind when you change between these chords, so that you can minimize the amount of finger movement you make – this will make changing between the chords easier and quicker.

Major Chords

Begin by playing four downstrums on a G major chord then, without stopping, move your fingers to D major and play another four strums. Repeat the sequence from the beginning by changing back to G major. Try to keep an even tempo throughout and practise slowly until you are able to change between the chords without pausing or hesitating. Notice how the third finger stays at the third fret for both G and D major. Use this as a pivot point to lead the chord change. Try to move all three fretting fingers as one shape when changing chord, rather than placing the fingers on one at a time; this will make the chord changes smoother.

Combining Chords

Once you feel fully familiar with the four chord shapes, try and combine them in this four-chord sequence, playing four downstrums for each chord.

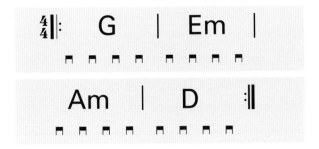

1. Look for any links between the different chord fingerings so that you can minimize the amount of finger movement you need to make.

2. Remember to place the fingers for each complete chord shape on the fretboard together, rather than finger by finger.

3. Practise very slowly so that you don't develop a habit of slowing down or stopping between chord changes.

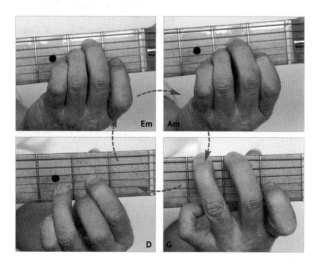

Strumming

Strumming chords forms the foundation of any guitar player's range of techniques. Strumming can be used to accompany your own or someone else's singing; it can also be used to provide a backing for lead-guitar playing. Being able to strum in a variety of styles will enable you to play rhythm guitar in a wide range of musical genres.

Strumming is an essential technique to master.

Strum Technique

For the music to flow smoothly it's essential to develop a relaxed strumming action. It will aid the fluency of rhythm playing if the the action comes from the wrist: a fluid and easy strumming action is best achieved this way, with the wrist loose and relaxed. If the wrist is stiff and not allowed to move freely then excessive arm movement will occur, as the strumming action will be forced to come from the elbow instead. As this can never move as fluently as the wrist, there will be a loss of smoothness and rhythmic potential.

Strumming Exercises

1. Begin by strumming an E minor chord using four downstrums per measure, and then experiment by inserting a quick upstrum between the second and third beats. The upstrum should be played by an upwards movement generated from the wrist, as though the strumming hand is almost effortlessly

bouncing back into position ready for the next downstrum. Keep practising this technique until it feels natural, always making sure that the arm itself isn't moving up and down when you're strumming.

$\frac{4}{4}$ ‖ Em | Em ‖

⊓ ⊓ ⊓ ⊓   ⊓ ⊓ V ⊓ ⊓
1 2 3 4   1 2 & 3 4

EXERCISE 1

2. Progress to adding two upstrums per bar: one between beats two and three, and one after the fourth beat. After the first two bars, try changing the chord to A minor and see if you can keep the strumming pattern going. If you can't change the chord quickly enough then start again from the beginning, playing at a much slower tempo.

3. To really get the strumming hand moving try adding an upstrum after every downstrum. Although this strumming style would be too busy

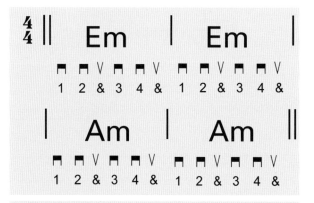

EXERCISE 2

for most songs, this exercise does provide practice in building a fluent strumming technique. Make sure that you have the plectrum positioned correctly, with its tip extending only just beyond the index fingertip, so that it does not drag on the strings as you strum.

EXERCISE 3

57

Finger-picking

Finger-picking can provide a really interesting
alternative to strumming. The technique is not just
confined to classical or folk guitarists – many rock
and pop players also use finger-picking as a method of
bringing melodic interest to a chord progression and
as a way of introducing musical subtleties to a song.

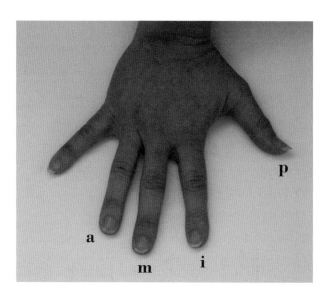

In music notation, each picking finger is identified by a letter: '**p**' represents the thumb, '**i**' the index finger, '**m**' the middle finger and '**a**' the third finger. (As it is much shorter than the others, the little finger is rarely used in finger-picking.)

Tip
It's easier to finger-pick if you let your fingernails grow a little. Using nails to pick the strings will also give you a crisper, clearer and stronger sound.

The thumb is mostly used for playing the bass strings (the lowest three strings), while the fingers are used for playing the treble strings. There are many different ways of finger-picking, but one of the easiest is to use the 'a' finger for picking the first string, the 'm' finger for the second string and the 'i' finger for the third string.

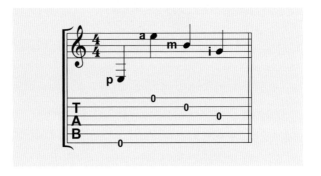

Picking Patterns

Many guitarists use a repetitive finger-picking pattern throughout a song to create a continuity of sound. Picking patterns nearly always begin by playing the root note of the chord (i.e. the note that gives the letter name to the chord) on the bass string using the thumb. For example, the low E string would be the first note of a pattern when finger-picking on a chord of E minor, and the open A string would be the first note when finger-picking on a chord of A minor.

If the picking pattern on a chord is repeated then sometimes a different bass is used the second time. This will normally be another note from the chord, usually the adjacent bass string. This technique can completely transform a simple chord progression, making it sound quite complex because of the moving bass line. This style of finger-picking is known as 'alternating bass'.

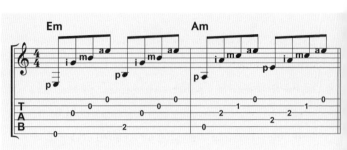

In some musical styles, more complex picking patterns might be used on the treble strings. It is best to practise these types of patterns on one chord until the picking pattern feels totally comfortable. Once you are familiar with a pattern it's relatively easy to apply it to a chord progression. You just need to take care about which bass note to pick on each chord, ensuring you use the root note as your starting point.

More Chords

The more chords you learn, the more songs you'll be able to play. Developing knowledge of even just the 10 most common chords will enable you to play literally thousands of songs, providing you practise them enough so that you can change fluently from chord to chord.

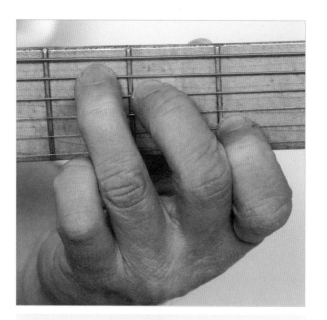

C major is one of the simplest chords to learn.

Main Chord Types

Although there are dozens of different chord types, all of these can be considered just variations of the two core types of chords: major chords and minor chords.

For example, if you come across a chord chart that includes Am7, playing a simple A minor chord will work almost as well.

Developing a good knowledge of the most popular major and minor chords will provide a firm foundation for all future chord playing.

Major Chords

In addition to the G and D major chords that were covered on pages 48 and 49, some other important major chords to start with are A, C, E and F.

A

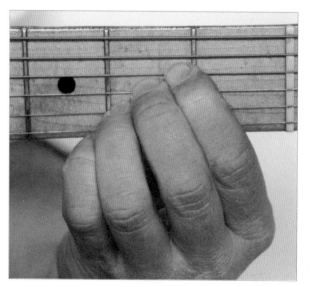

1
2
3
4
5
6
7
8
9
10
11
12

C

E

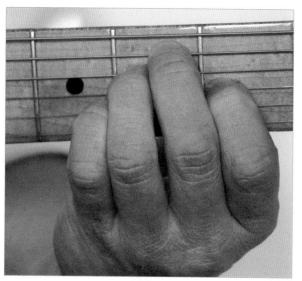

F

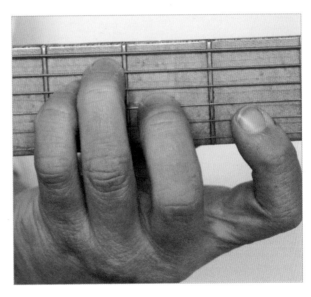

Notice that all the strings can be strummed on the E major chord, whereas the sixth string should be omitted when the A or C chords are strummed.

The F major chord is different from the other chord fingerings in that the first finger needs to lie flat across both the first and second strings. You will find this easier if you ensure that your thumb is positioned quite low at the back of the guitar neck; this will help you keep your first finger flat while the second and third fingers press with the fingertips. Make sure that you only strum the top four strings when playing the F major chord.

Minor Chords

In addition to the Em and Am chords that were covered on pages 46 and 47, the other most important minor chords to learn at first are Dm and F♯m.

1
2
3
4
5
6
7
8
9
10
11
12

Dm

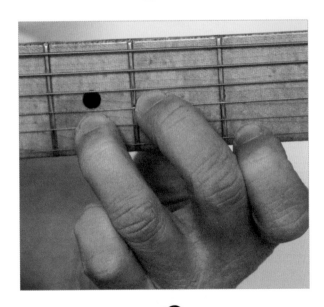

70

F♯m

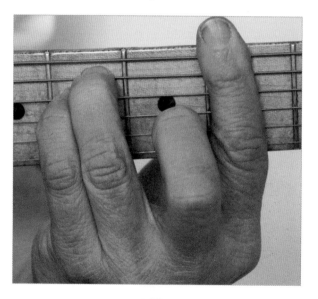

Both Dm and F♯m are four-string chords (i.e. the fifth and sixth strings should be omitted when playing these chords). The F♯m chord is a development of the technique that you gained when learning to play the F major chord, but this time the first finger needs to fret all the top three strings.

If you find this tricky, you might like to try resting the second finger on top of the first finger; this will add extra weight and strength to help the first finger hold down all three strings. Positioning the fretting finger as close as possible to the fretwire will reduce the amount of finger pressure required.

Keys

The 'key' of a song refers to its overall tonality, and dictates which scale will be used as the basis of the melody and which chords fit naturally into the arrangement. Understanding which chords go together in a key will help you work out the chord structure of songs, and will provide a framework to begin writing your own songs.

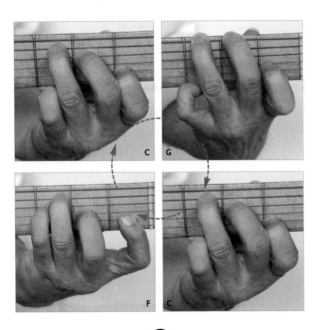

Major Keys

In each major key, three major chords occur –
as shown below:

Key	Major Chords in the Key
C major	C F G
G major	G C D
D major	D G A
A major	A D E

A song or chord progression will normally begin with
the tonic (keynote) chord. This is the chord that has
the same name as the key. For example, in the key
of C major, C is the tonic (keynote) chord.

Minor chords also occur in major keys. Some of the
most commonly used minor chords in the keys of
C, D, E, F and G major are shown below.

Key	Minor Chords in the Key		
C major	Dm	Em	Am
G major	Am	Bm	Em
D major	Em	F#m	Bm
A major	Bm	Dm	F#m
E major	F#m	G#m	C#m

Although there are no fixed rules about which chords can be combined when you are composing a song or chord progression, if you select chords from the same key they will always fit together well. Below is an example of a chord progression using chords in the key of C major.

‖ C | Dm | Em | F |
Am | G | F | C ‖

Chord progression in the key of C major.

Minor Keys

In each minor key, three minor chords are closely
related, and most commonly occur in popular songs.
For example, in the key of A minor the chords of Am,
Dm and Em are the most important.

Am   Dm   Em

Three major chords also occur in each minor key.
For example, in the key of A minor, C, F and G major
chords occur. As all these chords are within the
same key they can be combined in any order (after
starting with the tonic/keynote chord) to make a
pleasant-sounding chord sequence.

An example is shown on the following page, but
you can experiment with rearranging the chords in
a different order and then playing them through to
hear the musical result.

Simple Chord Progressions

|| Am | F | G | C |
Am | Dm | Em | Am ||

Chord progression in the key of A minor.

|| G | D | C | G |
Em | Am | D | G ||

Chord progression in the key of G major.

‖ D | Em | F#m | Em |
G | A | G | D ‖

Chord progression in the key of D major.

‖ C | G | Am | Am |
F | Em | Dm | C ‖

Chord progression in the key of C major.

‖ A │ E │ F#m │ E │
D │ E │ A │ A ‖

Chord progression in the key of A major.

‖ Em │ D │ C │ D │
Am │ G │ D │ Em ‖

Chord progression in the key of E minor.

1
2
3
4
5
6
7
8
9
10
11
12

The Basics

This is where you get into the nuts
and bolts of playing the electric guitar.
To be a good player, you must be able
to play in time. It is also important to
be able to read rhythm notation, chord
charts and rhythm charts. Another
basic essential is to be able to strum
well. All of these elements combined
will help you start to produce
a great sound.

Timing

The most important skill any rhythm-guitar player needs is the ability to maintain an even tempo and keep in time with other band members. It's essential that your rhythm playing sits in the same groove as the other members of the rhythm section.

Developing Timing Skills

Some people have a natural sense of rhythm and timing that just needs nurturing, while others have to concentrate on developing a secure sense of timing. A simple test to evaluate your sense of timing is to try and clap along to a recording by one of your favourite bands. While listening to the recording, focus your attention on the drums and try to clap a regular beat that matches the main rhythmic pulses within the song. Listen carefully to your clapping and see if you can stay in time throughout the whole song – .stamina is an important aspect of rhythm playing. Before you try to play through a song make sure that you have mastered any technical challenges, such as awkward chord changes, in advance. Otherwise, the temptation will be to slow down when approaching the difficult bits and perhaps speed up on the easy bits. You should try to avoid developing poor timing habits from the start by always choosing a slow practice tempo at which you can master the whole

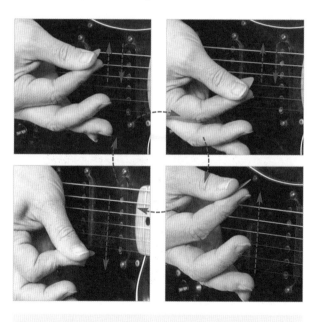

Keeping strict time is critical, even when varying the technique. Here, two quick alternating strums are followed by a full upstroke across all strings, then a solid downstroke.

song – difficult bits and all! Once you can play the song without any mistakes or hesitations, it's relatively easy to gradually increase the tempo each time you practise.

Timing Aids

Ideally you should always try to practise your rhythm playing with a device that keeps regular time. The simplest method is to practise with a metronome. This is a small mechanical or electronic device that

Metronomes are now available in traditional and electronic forms (pictured).

sounds a click on each beat. You can set it to click in increments from a very slow to a super-fast tempo. It's always best to practise anything new at a slow tempo, increasing the metronome setting by a couple of notches each time you've successfully played it the whole way through.

A drum machine can be used instead of a metronome. The advantage of the drum machine is that you can set it to play back interesting drum patterns to help inspire your strumming style. You can programme the machine, or use preset patterns, so that it emulates different musical genres.

Playing along to records is also a good method of developing a secure sense of timing: the band on the recording won't wait around if you lose time or hesitate over a chord change. Because there will be a longer space between beats, playing along with songs at a slow tempo emphasizes any timing inconsistencies – so don't forget to practise a few ballads alongside the thrash metal!

1
2
3
4
5
6
7
8
9
10
11
12

Time Signatures

The time signature is the most important element in setting the musical feel and mood of a piece of music. It provides the framework for the rhythmic structure of a song and plays a large part in establishing the character of the music.

Recognizing Time Signatures

The symbol indicating the time signature is always written at the start of the music or chord chart. The time signature is normally written as two numbers, one above the other. The top number represents the number of beats per measure (bar), while the bottom number refers to the type of beats.

The most common time signature used in all styles of popular music is $\frac{4}{4}$ time. This indicates that there are four beats in a measure, and that these are quarter notes (crotchets). Sometimes the $\frac{4}{4}$ symbol is replaced with **C**, meaning 'common time'.

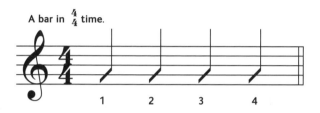

A bar in $\frac{4}{4}$ time.

1   2   3   4

Note that the time signature only tells you the number and type of 'beats' that will occur in a measure; this is not the same as the number of 'notes' you can play in the measure. For example, a measure of music in $\frac{4}{4}$ time will last for the equivalent duration of four quarter beats, but in this space you might play less longer-lasting notes or more shorter notes. In fact, you can play any combination of long, medium or short notes providing the duration per measure is equivalent to four quarter-note beats. (See pages 91-95 for more information on understanding rhythm notation.)

Other Commonly Used

Time Signatures

$\frac{2}{4}$: this has two quarter-note beats per measure. This time signature tends to give a march-like feel to the music.

$\frac{3}{4}$: this has three quarter-note beats per measure. This time signature gives a waltz-like character to the music and is often used in country and folk ballads.

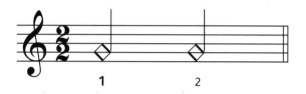

$\frac{2}{2}$: this has two half-note beats per measure. This is equivalent in length to $\frac{4}{4}$ time, but with two long beats per measure instead of four quarter-note beats.

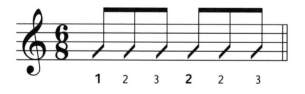

$\frac{6}{8}$: this has six eighth-note beats per measure. However, these are normally played as two groups of three.

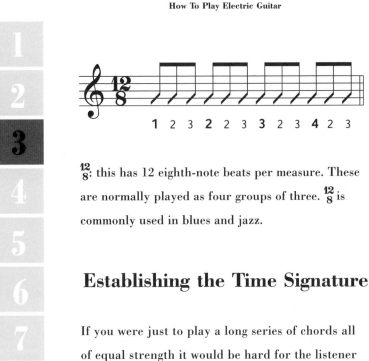

$\frac{12}{8}$: this has 12 eighth-note beats per measure. These are normally played as four groups of three. $\frac{12}{8}$ is commonly used in blues and jazz.

Establishing the Time Signature

If you were just to play a long series of chords all of equal strength it would be hard for the listener to recognize any rhythmic structure in the music – in other words, they wouldn't be able to 'feel the groove'. So normally the first beat of each measure is slightly accented, as this helps the sense of rhythm in a piece of music. In $\frac{6}{8}$ and $\frac{12}{8}$ time, an accent is normally played on the first of each group of three notes. (If you're playing in a band it might be the drums or other instruments that emphasize these accents.)

Rhythm Notation

Understanding how rhythms are written down will help you play through notated chord charts. The ability to notate your own rhythms is useful for passing the information to other players and as a memory aid. Even if you intend to rely mainly on tablature, a knowledge of rhythm notation will help you get the most out of the many song transcriptions that provide the full notation with the tab.

Note Values

Rhythm notation consists of pitchless notes and rests. The type of note used tells you how many beats a chord lasts; the type of rest used tells you how many beats a silence lasts. The diagram below shows the names of the most common types of notes, their symbols and how many of each type of note can occur in a single measure in $\frac{4}{4}$ time.

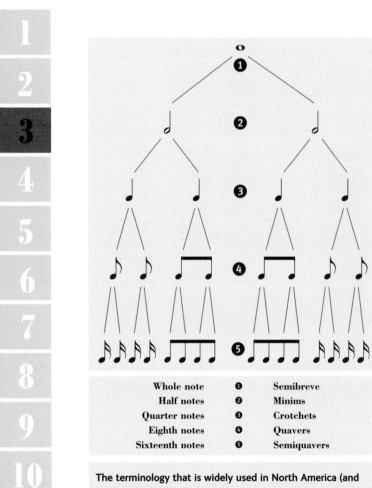

Whole note	❶	Semibreve
Half notes	❷	Minims
Quarter notes	❸	Crotchets
Eighth notes	❹	Quavers
Sixteenth notes	❺	Semiquavers

The terminology that is widely used in North America (and increasingly amongst pop, rock and jazz musicians in the UK and elsewhere) is different from that traditionally used by classical musicians in many parts of the world. In the key above the modern names are shown on the left and the traditional names are shown on the right.

Rests

The table below shows the names of the most common
types of rests, their symbols, their note equivalents,
and the duration of each type of rest in $\frac{4}{4}$ time.

Name	Rest symbol	Note equivalent	Duration in $\frac{4}{4}$ time
semibreve rest (whole rest)	▬	◇	4 beats
minim rest (half rest)	▬	◇	2 beats
crotchet rest (quarter rest)	𝄽	♩	1 beat
quaver rest (eighth rest)	𝄾	♪	1/2 beat
semiquaver rest (16th rest)	𝄿	♬	1/4 beat

Dotted Notes

A dot after a note or rest means that the note or rest
lasts for half as long again. This chart shows the
values of dotted notes and dotted rests in $\frac{4}{4}$ time.

Name	Note	Rest	Duration in time
dotted minim (dotted half note)			3 beats
dotted crotchet (dotted quarter note)			1 1/2 beats
dotted quaver (dotted eighth note)			3/4 of a beat

Ties

A curved line known as a 'tie' is used to join together two notes of the same pitch in order to increase the duration of the note.

In this example, the first chord would be allowed to sustain for the equivalent of five eighth notes. It is not possible to use a dot after the initial chord as this would have increased the duration of the note to the equivalent of six eighth notes.

Another common instance where ties are used is across bar lines as a method of sustaining a note beyond the end of a measure.

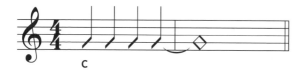

In this example, a tie is used so that the chord at the end of measure one can sustain into measure two.

Triplets

A triplet sign indicates where three notes should be played in the space of two notes of the same value.

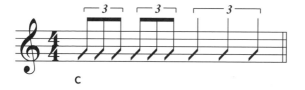

Chord Charts

Simple chord charts are the most commonly used way of notating the chord structure of a song or progression. If you audition for a pop or rock band, the music you'll be asked to play will most likely be presented as a simple chord chart.

Reading Chord Charts

A chord chart normally has the time signature written at the very beginning. If there is no time signature then it's usually safe to assume that the music is in $\frac{4}{4}$ time.

Each measure is separated by a vertical line, with two vertical lines indicating the end of the piece. Chord symbols are used to show which chords should be played.

96

Split Measures

When more than one chord appears in a single measure it can be assumed that the measure is to be evenly divided between the chords that appear within it. In a song in $\frac{3}{4}$ time, if three chords all appear in the same measure then you can assume that the measure is to be divided equally – with one beat per chord.

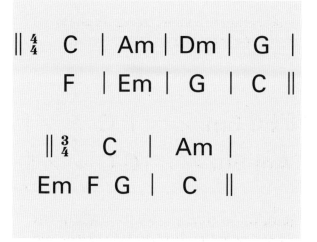

In the penultimate measure, each chord lasts for one beat.

In many chord charts, in order to make the intention clear and avoid confusion, any division within a measure is shown by either a dot or a diagonal line after each chord: each dot or diagonal line indicates another beat.

$$\| \; {\textstyle\frac{4}{4}} \; C \; \diagup \; Am \diagup \; | Dm \diagup \; G \; \diagup \; |$$
$$F \; \diagup \; Em \diagup \; | G \; \diagup \; C \; \diagup \; \|$$

Each chord lasts for two beats: one beat indicated by the chord symbol and an additional beat indicated by the diagonal line.

$$\| \; {\textstyle\frac{4}{4}} \; C \; Em \; \diagup \diagup \; | \; F \; G \; \diagup \; \diagup \; |$$
$$Am \; Em \diagup \; \diagup \; | G \; C \; \diagup \diagup \; \|$$

In this example, the first chord in each measure lasts for just one beat and the second chord lasts for three beats.

$$\| \frac{4}{4} C \ . \ . \ Dm \, | \, Em \ . \ . \ F \ |$$
$$Dm \ . \ . \ G \ | \, F \ . \ . \ C \, \|$$

In this example, instead of diagonal lines, dots are used to show the rhythmic divisions within each measure. The first chord in each measure lasts for three beats and the second chord lasts for one beat.

Interpreting Chord Charts

In standard chord charts, while the duration of each chord is clearly shown, the rhythm style that should be played is left to the discretion of the performer. In theory this means that you could interpret the chart in any way you wish in terms of the number of strums per beat, however you should make sure that your rhythm playing relates to the musical style and mood of the song.

Following Chord Charts

If every bar of a whole song were written out in a chord chart it would take up several pages and become cumbersome to read. Instead chord charts are normally abbreviated by using a number of 'repeat symbols'. In order to follow a chord chart accurately it is essential to understand what each repeat symbol means.

// $\frac{4}{4}$ Em / Am / D / Em /
G / C / D / D ://

When you write down your own chord charts make sure they are clear and easy to read. You'll need to go back to them later, or share them with others.

Repeat Symbols

The repeat symbol is used when one bar is to be repeated exactly.

∕.   This symbol is used when more than one bar is to be repeated.

∕∕.   The number of bars to be repeated is written above the symbol.

Here is an example of these symbols in use.

‖ $\frac{4}{4}$ G | ∕. | C | D |

$\overset{2}{∕∕.}$ | Em | ∕.   ‖

should be played as

‖ $\frac{4}{4}$ G | G | C | D |

   C | D | Em | Em ‖

Section Repeats

The symbol of a double bar-line followed by two dots indicates the start of a section, and the symbol of two dots followed by a double bar-line indicates the end of the section to be repeated. If there are no dots at the start of the section, then repeat the music from the beginning of the piece. If the section is to be repeated more than once, the number of times it is to be played is written above the last repeat symbol.

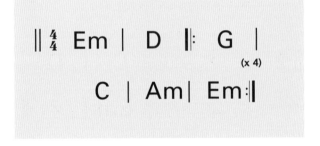

If two sections of music are identical, except for the last measure or measures, repeat dots are used in conjunction with first-time and second-time ending directions, as shown on the next page.

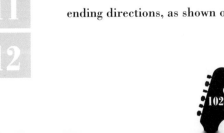

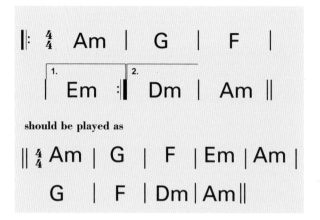

should be played as

As well as repeat dots there are several other commonly used repeat signs:

- **D.C.** (an abbreviation of *Da Capo*) means play 'from the beginning'. For example, if the entire piece of music is to be repeated, *D.C.* can be written at the end to instruct you to play it again from the beginning.

- **D.S.** (an abbreviation of *Dal Segno*) means play 'from the sign': . For example, if the verse and chorus of a song are to be repeated, but not the introduction, **D.S.** can be written at the end of the music with the D.S. sign written at the start of the verse. This instructs the performer to start again from the sign.

- **Coda** is the musical term for the end section of a piece of music. The start of the coda is marked by the sign: ⊕ .

- **Fine** is the musical term for the end of a piece of music.

Some of the above repeat signs might be combined in a chord chart.

Fine

‖ 4/4   Em | Am | D | Em ‖

D.C. al Fine

G | C | D | D ‖

In this example, after eight measures repeat from the beginning and then end after measure four where the sign 'Fine' appears.

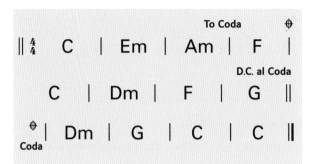

In this example above, after eight measures repeat from the beginning and then after measure four jump to the coda section.

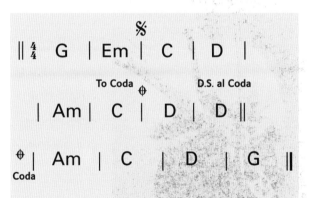

In this example above, after eight measures repeat from the start of measure three to the end of measure six, then jump to the coda section.

Rhythm Charts

While standard chord charts are commonly used by pop and rock bands, more detailed and complex charts known as 'rhythm charts' are often presented to guitarists involved in recording sessions and those

who play in theatre and function band settings. Learning to read rhythm charts will help expand your employability as a guitarist.

In a rehearsal studio, simple chord charts are a quick way of getting up to speed, but session guitarists need to understand rhythm charts provided by an arranger or producer.

Chart Styles

Some rhythm charts can be quite elaborate and
may include a fully notated rhythm part, as well
as detailed instructions about dynamics and tempo.
Others may contain notated rhythms only at the
beginning, in order to establish the feel of the song,
with further rhythm notation only being used where
specific rhythmic accents or features occur. The type
of rhythm charts you come across will depend on the
context and the transcriber's personal preferences.

Dynamic Markings

Symbols are often used in rhythm charts to indicate
changes in volume – e.g. when you should play softly
and when you should strum strongly. The symbols do
not refer to any precise decibel volume level, instead
their main function is to highlight changes in overall
volume. The most common dynamic markings are
shown below. Accents, where certain individual beats

are played stronger than others, are marked by this sign: >. The letters 'sfz' (sforzando) may be also used to indicate an accent.

Symbol	Name	Meaning
pp	pianissimo	very soft
p	piano	soft
mp	mezzo-piano	medium soft
mf	mezzo-forte	medium loud
f	forte	loud
ff	fortissimo	very loud
————	crescendo	getting louder
————	diminuendo	getting softer

Tempo

Most rhythm charts will contain an indication of the speed at which the music should be played; this is usually written at the start of the music. The tempo indication may appear in either traditional Italian musical terms or their English equivalents.

Alternatively, a metronome marking may be shown to indicate the exact number of beats per minute (b.p.m.). The most common tempos are shown in the table below.

Italian Term	Meaning	Approx speed
Largo	very slow	40–60 b.p.m.
Adagio	slow	50–75 b.p.m.
Andante	walking pace	75–100 b.p.m.
Moderato	moderate tempo	100–120 b.p.m.
Allegro	fast	120–160 b.p.m.
Presto	very quick	160–200 b.p.m.

Some music may contain changes in tempo. These are usually indicated through the use of Italian terms.

The most widely used are:

Italian Term	Meaning
Accel.	(an abbreviation of *accelerando*) means play gradually faster.
A tempo	indicates that you should resume the normal tempo after a deviation.
Meno mosso	(less movement) means that you should slow down at once.
Rall.	(an abbreviation of *rallentando*) means play gradually slower.
Rit.	(an abbreviation of *ritenuto*) means to hold back the tempo.

Playing Rhythm Charts

Below you'll see a sample rhythm chart, incorporating some of the terms and symbols described above. Refer to page 92 if you need to be reminded of the note values.

Strumming Patterns

Building up a repertoire of useful strumming patterns is a good way of developing your rhythm-guitar playing. Once you've mastered the core patterns used in rock and pop you can easily expand these by adding variations.

Strum Technique

Playing with a loose wrist action is an essential ingredient of developing a good strumming technique. Keeping the wrist tight and strumming by using the whole forearm will severely restrict the potential speed and fluency of your rhythm playing – so make sure that the strumming action comes from your wrist. It's a good idea to practise in front of a mirror, or record a video of yourself playing guitar, so that you can see if you're using the right technique.

Chord Technique

Be careful not to over-grip with the fretting-hand thumb on the back of the neck as this will cause muscle fatigue and tend to limit freedom of the thumb to move. The fretting-hand thumb must move freely when changing chords. If the thumb remains static

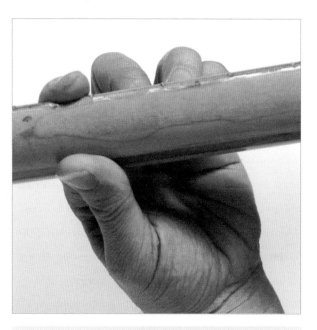

Make sure you hold the thumb in opposition to the fingers, behind the neck, but don't press too hard.

113

this restricts the optimum positioning of the fingers for the next chord, which may result in unnecessary stretching and the involuntary dampening of certain strings (as the fingers are not positioned upright on their tips). Be aware that for the fingers to move freely the wrist, elbow and shoulder must be flexible and relaxed. Make sure your standing or sitting position doesn't restrict the movement of your hands and arms.

Strum Patterns

On pages 115–17 you'll find several examples of popular strumming patterns. It's a good idea to start by playing all the progressions using just four downstrums per measure – this way you'll become familiar with the chord changes before tackling the strum patterns. In nearly all styles of music, there is no need to strum all the strings on every beat – feel free to add variety, particularly by omitting some bass strings on upstrokes and some treble strings on downstrokes.

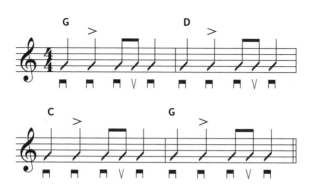

The second beat of the measure is accented to create
dynamic variety. An upstroke is used after the third beat
of the measure.

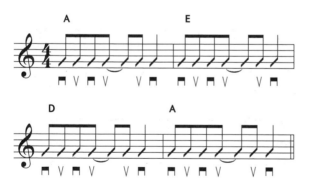

The pattern above uses a mixture of down- and upstrokes,
but notice how the fourth strum and the last strum are
held longer than the others. This variety creates an
effective rhythm.

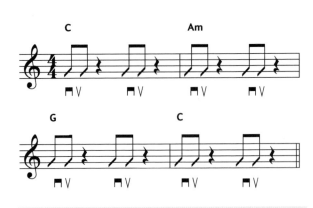

A simple down-up strum pattern (above), but the use of rests creates a very distinctive rhythmic effect.

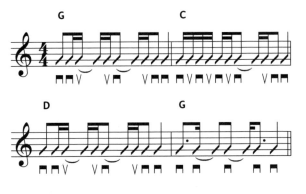

This 'Bo Diddley' type pattern is a good example of how to use rhythmic variations: notice that measures 1 and 3 are the same, while measures 2 and 4 are each variations on the first measure.

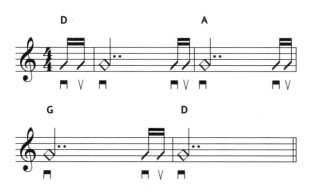

This typical rock strumming pattern is essentially just one strum per measure. What makes it distinctive is the rapid down-up 'pre-strum' before the main beat. These 'pre-strums' do not need to be played across all the strings, and open strings can be used on the second of them to help get to the main chord quickly.

4

Scales

Scales are the foundation of every good guitar solo. By learning how to connect your scales with chords, you will be able to make your musical ideas a reality. Just as scales are a cornerstone of a player's technique, so learning the basics of notation is essential for any guitarist. You will discover how to translate the notes on a page into wonderful music.

1

2

3

4

5

6

7

8

9

10

11

12

Basics of Notation

There are three ways in which scales, licks and solos are written down: traditional notation, tablature and fretboxes. (See page 44 for a more detailed description of fretboxes). While you don't need to be a great sight-reader to play lead guitar, having a good understanding of each of the notation systems will help you learn lead guitar relatively easily.

Tablature

Tablature (TAB) uses six lines to represent the six strings of the guitar, with the top line representing the high E string and the bottom line representing the low E string.

Numbers are written on the lines to indicate which fret to play at. A zero indicates that the string is played open. TAB is great for notating scales or

120

chords and, although it doesn't usually include any rhythm notation, its simplicity makes it ideal for learning music that you have heard before.

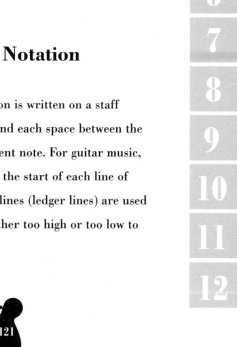

This means play at the third fret on the second string.

Music Notation

Traditional music notation is written on a staff of five lines. Each line, and each space between the lines, represents a different note. For guitar music, a treble clef is written at the start of each line of music. Temporary extra lines (ledger lines) are used for any notes that are either too high or too low to fit on the staff.

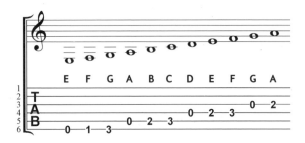

ABOVE: Notes on the spaces in the treble clef.

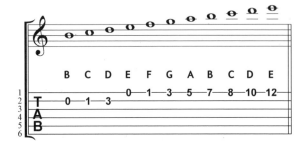

ABOVE: Using ledger lines, this diagram shows the notes from the open low E string to the E at the 12th fret on the first string.

A sharp sign (♯) is written in front of a note, on the same line or space, to raise its pitch by a half step (semitone) i.e. equivalent to one fret higher.

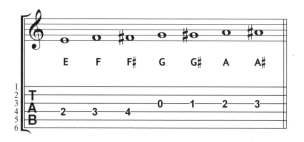

A flat sign (♭) is written in front of a note, on the same line or space, to lower its pitch by a half step (semitone). Any sharps or flats affect all the notes of the same pitch within the bar. A natural sign (♮) on the same line or space is used to cancel the previous sharp or flat.

123

Key Signatures

The key of a piece of music determines the main
notes that will be included in it. In music notation
a key signature is written at the beginning of every
line of music to indicate the key. Key signatures make
music easier to read because any sharps or flats in
the key need only be written at the start of each line
and will then apply to all those notes throughout the
piece, rather than needing to write a sharp or flat
sign every time such a note occurs. Each major key
has a unique key signature, consisting of a collection
of sharps or flats written in a set order; these sharps
and flats match those that occur in the major scale
for that key. The key of C major is unusual in that
no sharps or flats occur in the keyscale, and therefore
the key signature is blank.

Minor keys share key signatures with their relative
major keys (i.e. major keys that have a keynote three
half steps higher than that of the minor key).

124

| G major | D major | A major |
| E minor | B minor | F# minor |

| E major | B major | F# major |
| C# minor | G# minor | D# minor |

ABOVE: Sharp key signatures

| F major | B♭ major | E♭ major |
| D minor | D minor | C minor |

| A♭ major | D♭ major | G♭ major |
| F minor | D minor | E♭ minor |

ABOVE: Flat key signatures

Major Scales

By far the most important scale in music is the major scale. All other scales, and even all chords, can be considered as stemming from the major scale. The major scale is used as the basis for the majority of popular melodies. When used in lead playing it gives a bright and melodic sound.

Scale Construction

The major scale is constructed by using a standard combination of whole steps/whole tones (W) and half steps/semitones (H).

C	plus a **whole** step	=	D
D	plus a **whole** step	=	E
E	plus a **half** step	=	F
F	plus a **whole** step	=	G
G	plus a **whole** step	=	A
A	plus a **whole** step	=	B
B	plus a **half** step	=	C

Regardless of the key, the pattern of tones and semitones is as follows:

W W H W W W H

For example, the **C major scale** is constructed as follows:

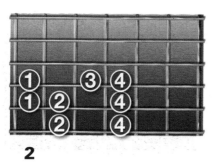

C major scale.

Transposing Scales

All the scales illustrated in this chapter are 'transpositional': they can be played in other keys simply by starting the finger pattern at a different fret.

4

D major scale.

For example, to play the D major scale, use the exact fingering shown for C major but start two frets higher. For some keys, for example G major, you might prefer to start the scale pattern on the low E string in order to avoid high fingerboard positions.

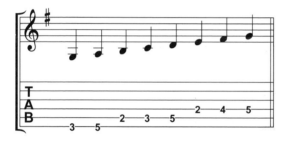

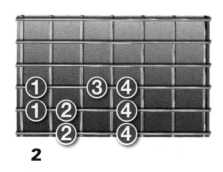

G major scale.

Pentatonic Major Scale

The term 'pentatonic' means 'five-note'; the
pentatonic major scale is a five-note abbreviation of
the standard major scale, with the fourth and seventh
degrees of the major scale omitted. For example, the
notes in the C major scale are C D E F G A B.

2

C pentatonic major scale.

To convert this into the C pentatonic major scale omit the notes F (the 4th) and B (the 7th), resulting in C D E G A.

The pentatonic major scale has none of the overtly sugary sound often associated with the standard major scale – instead it has a great combination of brightness with a cutting edge. It is a very useful scale for improvising in major keys; because it contains fewer notes than the standard major scale there is less chance of any of the notes clashing with the accompanying chords.

Traditionally, pentatonic major scales have been used in country music, but many rock bands – from the Rolling Stones and Free to Travis and Supergrass – have used them frequently on their recordings. Brit-rock bands were great fans of the pentatonic major scale, particularly Noel Gallagher, who relied on them almost exclusively for his solos on the first few Oasis albums. Some of its greatest exponents are country-rock players like Albert Lee and Danny Gatton.

131

Minor Scales

There are a variety of minor scales to suit all musical styles, from the soulful natural minor scale to the exotic harmonic minor scale. But it is the rock-edged pentatonic minor scale that is by far the most widely used scale in lead-guitar playing.

Natural Minor Scale

The natural minor scale is constructed using a standard combination, regardless of the key, of

C	plus a **whole** step	=	D
D	plus a **half** step	=	E♭
E♭	plus a **whole** step	=	F
F	plus a **whole** step	=	G
G	plus a **half** step	=	A♭
A♭	plus a **whole** step	=	B♭
B♭	plus a **whole** step	=	C

whole steps/tones (W) and half steps/semitones (H) in the following pattern:

W H W W H W W

For example, **C natural minor scale** is constructed as follows:

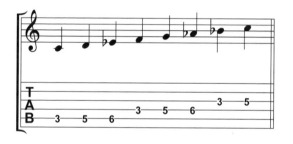

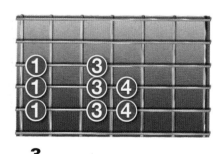

3

C natural minor scale.

133

The interval spelling for the natural minor scale is 1 2 ♭3 4 5 ♭6 ♭7 8, meaning that, in comparison to the major scale with the same keynote, the third, sixth and seventh notes are flattened by a half step. The natural minor scale is widely used in rock- and blues-based music. The scale has a soulful, yet melodic sound. Carlos Santana and Gary Moore are two of its best-known exponents.

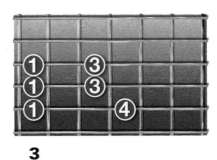

C pentatonic minor scale.

Pentatonic Minor Scale

In all forms of rock music, the pentatonic minor scale is the most commonly used scale for lead-guitar playing. The interval spelling is 1 ♭3 4 5 ♭7 8. It is a popular scale for improvising in minor keys because it contains fewer notes than the natural minor scale – this makes the scale easy to use and means that there is little chance of any of the notes clashing with the accompanying chords.

Harmonic Minor Scale

The harmonic minor scale is very similar to the natural minor scale (see the next page for fingerings and notation). The only difference is that, in the harmonic minor scale, the note on the seventh degree is raised by a half step. This results in a large interval between the sixth and seventh degrees of the scale, giving the scale its distinctive, exotic sound.

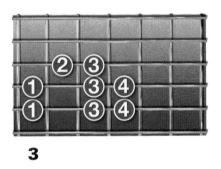

3

C harmonic minor scale.

The interval spelling is 1 2 ♭3 4 5 ♭6 7 8. Ritchie Blackmore was one of the first rock guitarists to exploit the melodic potential of this scale.

Melodic Minor Scale

The step pattern of this scale alters depending on whether it is being played ascending or descending.

136

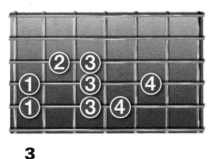

3

C melodic minor scale ascending.

When played descending it has the same notes as the natural minor scale; when played ascending the sixth and seventh degrees are each raised by a half step. The interval spelling is 1 2 ♭3 4 5 6 7 8 ascending and 1 2 ♭3 4 5 ♭6 ♭7 8 descending. The scale is mostly used in jazz rock and fusion.

1
2
3
4
5
6
7
8
9
10
11
12

5

Chords

In this section we look at chords.
Along with scales, chords form the
foundation of any guitarist's playing. In
order to play chords easily it is good to
understand intervals, the building
blocks of chords. You will then progress
on to simple chord construction. Once
you have mastered these foundation
chords and move on to more advanced
chords, you will quickly realize that
these are simply variations or
extensions of the basic chord types.

Intervals

Intervals are the spaces between notes from the major scale, or other scales. Chords are constructed by combining various intervals. The name of a chord is often based upon the largest interval contained within that chord.

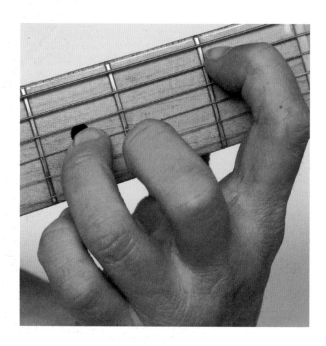

Major Second

A major second is the interval from the first to the second note of the major scale (e.g. in the key of C, from C to D).

Major Second

If you play the major second note an octave higher it forms a major ninth interval. This interval is included in all major ninth, minor ninth and dominant ninth chords.

Major Ninth

Major Third

A major third is the interval from the first to the
third note of the major scale (e.g. in the key of C,
from C to E). This interval is important in that it
defines the tonality of a chord; a chord that is
constructed with a major third interval from its
root note will always be a type of major chord.

Major Third

If you lower the major third interval by a half step it
becomes a minor third. Just as the major third interval
determines that a chord has a major tonality, the
minor third interval determines that a chord is minor.

Minor Third

Perfect Fourth

A perfect fourth is the interval from the first to the fourth note of the major scale (e.g. in the key of C, from C to F).

Perfect Fourth

Perfect Fifth

A perfect fifth is the interval from the first to the fifth note of the major scale (e.g. in the key of C, from C to G). The perfect fifth occurs in nearly all chords, apart from diminished or augmented chords.

Perfect Fifth

If you lower the perfect fifth interval by a half step it becomes a diminished (flattened) fifth. This interval occurs in diminished chords and any chords labelled with a flattened fifth note.

144

Diminished Fifth

If you raise the perfect fifth interval by a half step it becomes an augmented (sharpened) fifth. This interval occurs in augmented chords and any chords labelled with a sharpened fifth note

Augmented Fifth

Major Sixth

A major sixth is the interval from the first to the sixth note of the major scale (e.g. in the key of C, from C to A). The major sixth occurs in both major and minor sixth chords.

If you add an octave to a major sixth it becomes a major 13th interval. This interval is used in all 13th chords.

Major Sixth

Major 13th

Major Seventh

A major seventh is the interval from the first to the seventh note of the major scale (e.g. in the key of C, from C to B). The major seventh interval occurs in major seventh chords.

If you lower the major seventh interval by a half step it becomes a minor seventh. This interval occurs in both minor seventh and dominant seventh chords.

Major Seventh

Minor Seventh

Major Triads

Chords that contain three different notes are known as 'triads'. All standard major chords are triads. All other chords, no matter how elaborate, can be considered simply as variations or extensions of these triads. Therefore, learning all the major triads will provide a firm foundation for learning any other chords.

The first, third and fifth notes of the major scale make up a major triad. For example, the C major triad is formed by taking the first, third and fifth notes of the C major scale.

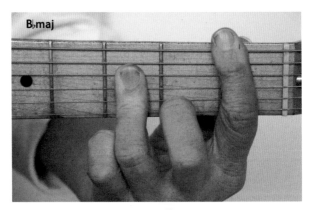

B♭maj

You can work out which notes are in **any major triad** by selecting the **first, third** and **fifth** notes from the major scale with the same starting note as the chord. This would give the following results:

			C Major Scale				
1	2	**3**	4	**5**	6	7	8
C	D	**E**	F	**G**	A	B	C

C Major Triad

C		**E**		**G**			

C	G	D	A
Major Triad	Major Triad	Major Triad	Major Triad
C E G	G B D	D F♯ A	A C♯ E
Notes in Triad	Notes in Triad	Notes in Triad	Notes in Triad

E	B	F♯	F
Major Triad	Major Triad	Major Triad	Major Triad
E G♯ B	B D♯ F♯	F♯ A♯ C♯	F A C
Notes in Triad	Notes in Triad	Notes in Triad	Notes in Triad

B♭	E♭	A♭	D♭
Major Triad	Major Triad	Major Triad	Major Triad
B♭ D F	E♭ G B♭	A♭ C E♭	D♭ F A♭
Notes in Triad	Notes in Triad	Notes in Triad	Notes in Triad

Although major triads only contain three different notes, strumming three-string chords could result in quite a thin sound, so quite often major chords are played with some of the notes doubled so that five or six strings can be strummed.

For example, in the open position G major chord below, the G note is played three times (on the sixth, third and first strings), the B note is played twice (on the fifth and second strings) and the D note is played once.

G   G Major
1st (G), 3rd (B), 5th (D)

Now that you know the notes contained in each major triad you can devise as many different fingerings for each chord as you wish. To help you get started, there follows one fretbox example for each major triad.

150

A   A Major
1st (A), 3rd (C♯), 5th (E)

B♭/A♯   B♭ Major
1st (B♭), 3rd (D), 5th (F)

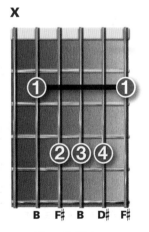

B   B Major
1st (B), 3rd (D♯), 5th (F♯)

C   C Major
1st (C), 3rd (E), 5th (G)

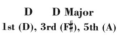

C#/Db   C# Major
1st (C#), 3rd (E#), 5th (G#)

D   D Major
1st (D), 3rd (F#), 5th (A)

Eb/D#   Eb Major
1st (Eb), 3rd (G), 5th (Bb)

E   E Major
1st (E), 3rd (G#), 5th (B)

F   F Major
1st (F), 3rd (A), 5th (C)

F♯/G♭   F♯ Major
1st (F♯), 3rd (A♯), 5th (C♯)

G   G Major
1st (G), 3rd (B), 5th (D)

A♭/G♯   A♭ Major
1st (A♭), 3rd (C), 5th (E♭)

153

Minor Triads

Minor triads have a more mellow, mournful sound than major triads but, just like major triads, they also contain only three different notes. All other minor chords are built on the foundation of these minor triads, so learning at least the most common minor triads is essential for any rhythm-guitar player.

Minor triads contain the first, flattened third and fifth notes of the major scale. (The flattened third note can be found one fret lower than the major third note.) For example, the C minor triad contains the notes C, E♭ and G. Taking the first, third and fifth notes from the natural minor scale will give the same results.

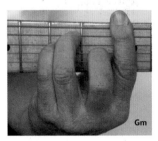

Gm

You can work out which notes are in **any minor triad** by selecting the **first**, **third** and **fifth** notes from the natural

minor scale with the same starting note as the chord. Remember that although triads consist of only three different notes, you can repeat one or more of the notes when playing them as chords on the guitar.

C Natural Minor Scale							
1	2	**3**	4	**5**	6	7	8
C	D	**E♭**	F	**G**	A♭	B♭	C

C Minor Triad		
C	**E♭**	**G**

Am	**Em**	**Bm**	**F♯m**
Minor Scale	Minor Scale	Minor Scale	Minor Scale
A C E	**E G B**	**B D F♯**	**F♯ A C♯**
Notes in Triad	Notes in Triad	Notes in Triad	Notes in Triad

C♯m	**G♯m**	**D♯m**	**Dm**
Minor Scale	Minor Scale	Minor Scale	Minor Scale
C♯ E G♯	**G♯ B D♯**	**D♯ F♯ A♯**	**D F A**
Notes in Triad	Notes in Triad	Notes in Triad	Notes in Triad

Gm	**Cm**	**Fm**	**B♭m**
Minor Scale	Minor Scale	Minor Scale	Minor Scale
G B♭ D	**C E♭ G**	**F A♭ C**	**B♭ D♭ F**
Notes in Triad	Notes in Triad	Notes in Triad	Notes in Triad

X O O

A E A C E

Am   A Minor
1st (A), ♭3rd (C), 5th (E)

X

B♭ F B♭ D♭ F

B♭m/A♯m   B♭ Minor
1st (B♭), ♭3rd (D♭), 5th (F)

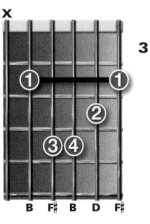

X

B F♯ B D F♯

Bm   B Minor
1st (B), ♭3rd (D), 5th (F♯)

X

3

C G C E♭ G

Cm   C Minor
1st (C), ♭3rd (E♭), 5th (G)

X

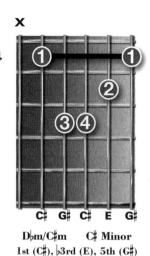

C♯ G♯ C♯ E G♯

D♭m/C♯m C♯ Minor
1st (C♯), ♭3rd (E), 5th (G♯)

X X O

D A D F

Dm D Minor
1st (D), ♭3rd (F), 5th (A)

X X

E♭ B♭ E♭ G♭

E♭m/D♯m E♭ Minor
1st (E♭), ♭3rd (G♭), 5th (B♭)

O   O O O

E B E G B E

Em E Minor
1st (E), ♭3rd (G), 5th (B)

Fm   F Minor
1st (F), ♭3rd (A♭), 5th (C)

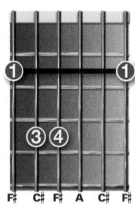

F♯m/G♭m   F♯ Minor
1st (F♯), ♭3rd (A), 5th (C♯)

Gm   G Minor
1st (G), ♭3rd (B♭), 5th (D)

A♭m/G♯m   A♭ Minor
1st (A♭), ♭3rd (C♭), 5th (E♭)

Other Triads

As well as major and minor triads, there are other triads: diminished, augmented and suspended (see pages 164–77). There are also some chords, known as 'diads', that contain only two different notes (see 'Fifth Chords' pages 164–65).

C F G C F

Csus4 C Suspended 4th
1st (C), 4th (F), 5th (G)

C E G♯ C E

C+ C Augmented
1st (C), 3rd (E), ♯5th (G♯)

Chord Construction

When you've studied the basic major and minor chords on the previous pages, you'll find that there's good news: all other chords can be viewed as variations or extensions of the basic chords. To convert the basic triads into other chords, all that's normally required is to add to the triad a note from the major scale.

Sixth Chords

To work out how to play any major sixth chord you just play through the major scale until you reach the sixth note in the scale. Find the name of this note and then add this note to the basic major triad – thereby converting it into a major sixth chord. For example, to play A major 6 (A6) you should add F♯ (the sixth note of the A major scale) to the A major chord. (You will find an F♯ note on the second fret of the first string.)

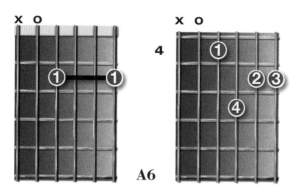

A6

Minor sixth chords are formed in the same way, by adding the sixth note of the major scale to the minor triad. Notice that you always use the major scale – even if the chord is minor!

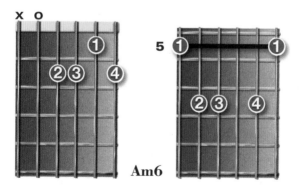

Am6

161

Seventh Chords

There are three main types of seventh chord: major seventh (maj7), dominant seventh (7) and minor seventh (m7). Only the major seventh chord uses the seventh note of the major scale; the other two types use the flattened seventh note of the scale.

The major seventh chord is formed by taking the basic major chord and adding the seventh note of the major scale to it. For example, Amaj7 contains the notes A C♯ E G♯.

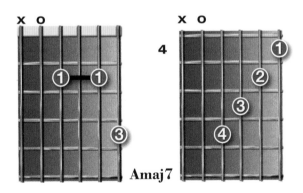

Amaj7

The dominant seventh chord is formed by taking the basic major chord and adding the flattened seventh note of the major scale to it. For example, A7 contains the notes A C♯ E G.

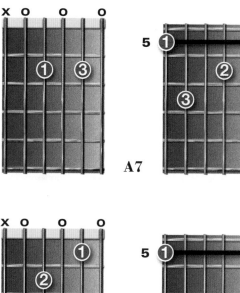

A7

Am7

The minor seventh chord is formed by taking the basic minor chord and adding the flattened seventh note of major scale to it. For example, Am7 contains the notes A C E G.

Asus4

Sus Chords

Some chords are formed by replacing a note, rather than adding one. Sus chords are a good example of this, as the chord's third is replaced by the fourth note of the major scale in sus4 chords, and by the second note of the scale in sus2 chords. For example, Asus2 contains the notes A B E, and Asus4 contains the notes A D E.

Fifth Chords

Fifth chords are unusual in that they do not include a major or minor third. They consist only of the root note and the fifth. For example, A5 contains the notes

A and E. In rock music, a prime example of the fifth chord is the 'power chord', in which the root note and the fifth above it are played on the sixth and fifth, or fifth and fourth strings. With the right combination of electric guitar, amp and effects, this powerful

sound characterizes hard rock and heavy metal.

A5

Tip

When adding notes to chords, it's normally best if you can find the note in a higher register, such as on the first string, before looking for it on the lower strings. Sometimes you might need to take a finger off a string to allow the new note to sound.

Extended & Altered Chords

Using extended chords, containing five or six notes, helps to create a rich sound and to extend your chordal vocabulary. Altered chords provide an ideal method of creating a sense of tension and adding harmonic dissonance to a chord progression.

Extended Chords

Just as seventh chords are built by adding an extra note to a basic triad, extended chords are built by adding one or more extra notes to a seventh chord. The most common types of extended chords are ninths, 11ths and 13ths. Each can be played in either a major, minor or dominant form.

166

Ninth Chords

Major ninth chords are extensions of major seventh chords. They are formed by adding the ninth note of the major scale (with the same starting note) to a major seventh chord. The interval spelling is 1 3 5 7 9. For example, Cmaj9 contains the notes C E G B (the notes of Cmaj7) plus the note of D (the ninth note of the C major scale). Major ninth chords have a delicate sound that makes them highly suitable for use in ballads.

Cmaj9

167

Dominant ninth chords are formed by adding the ninth note of the major scale to a dominant seventh chord. For example, C9 contains the notes C E G B♭ (the notes of C7) plus D (the ninth note of the C major scale). The interval spelling is 1 3 5 ♭7 9.

Dominant ninth chords have a rich, bluesy sound.

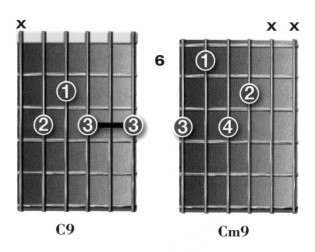

C9   Cm9

Minor ninth chords are extensions of minor seventh chords, formed by adding the ninth note of the major scale. For example, Cm9 contains C E♭ G B♭ (the notes of Cm7) plus D (the ninth note of the

C major scale). The interval spelling is 1 ♭3 5 ♭7 9.
Minor ninth chords have a suave, mellow sound
and are often used in soul and funk music.

Eleventh Chords

There are three main types of 11th chord as shown
here. You'll notice that each incorporates some form
of ninth chord, plus the 11th note of the major scale.
In practice, the ninth note is normally omitted when
playing 11th chords on the guitar.

Dominant 11th:	1 3 5 ♭7 9 11
Minor 11th:	1 ♭3 5 ♭7 9 11
Major 11th:	1 3 5 7 9 11

Cmaj11

C11

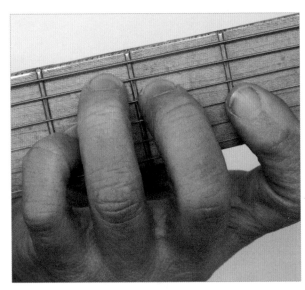

Cm11

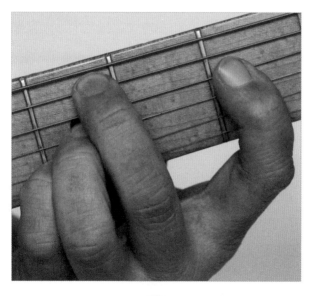

Cmaj11

Thirteenth Chords

There are three main types of 13th chord, as shown
in the table below. In practice, it is not possible
to play all seven notes of a 13th chord on guitar,
therefore some notes (normally the 9th, 11th and
sometimes the 5th) are omitted.

Dominant 13th:	1 3 5 ♭7 9 11 13
Minor 13th:	1 ♭3 5 ♭7 9 11 13
Major 13th:	1 3 5 7 9 11 13

Cmaj13

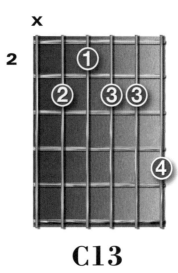

C13

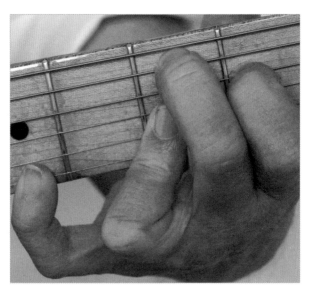

174

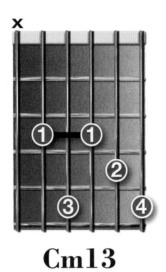

Cm13

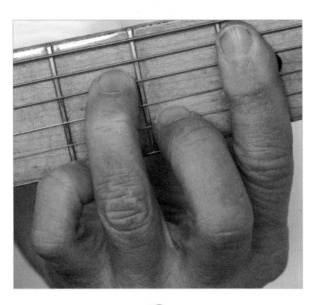

Cmaj13

Altered Chords

These are chords in which the fifth and/or ninth has been 'altered' – i.e. either raised or lowered by a half step. Altered chords are most commonly used in jazz. These are examples of commonly used altered chords.

Augmented triad:	1 3 ♯5
Diminished triad:	1 ♭3 ♭5
Diminished 7th chord:	1 ♭3 ♭5 ♭♭7
Dominant 7th ♭5:	1 3 ♭5 ♭7
Dominant 7th ♭9:	1 3 5 ♭7 ♭9
Dominant 7th ♯9:	1 3 5 ♭7 ♯9

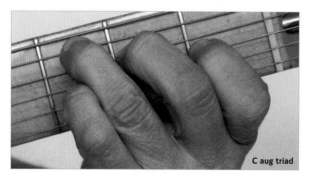

C aug triad

6

Basic Techniques

Now that you have begun to get to grips
with playing your guitar, it is time to
learn a few techniques that will enhance
your sound. Hammer-ons and pull-offs
will give your playing fluency, while
vibrato and string bends will enable
you to make your playing more
expressive. You will also learn slides,
string damping and plectrum skills.

String Damping

Nearly all rock and blues players use string damping as a way of controlling the guitar's volume and tone. By resting the side of the strumming hand lightly on the strings, close to the saddle, a choked or muted sound can be achieved by deadening the sustain of the strings.

Damping Technique

String damping is an essential technique for varying the tone and volume of your guitar playing. The technique can be used after a note or chord has been played to achieve a short and detached 'staccato' effect. Damping can also be used to bring out accents in a rhythm, by maintaining the muting effect throughout and releasing only intermittently on the beats to be accented.

Strumming-hand Damping

To learn this technique, first strum slowly across all the open strings to hear the natural sound of the guitar. Then, place your strumming hand at a 90-degree angle to the strings, close to the saddle, with the side of the hand (in line with the little finger) pressing lightly against all six strings. Maintain contact with the strings with the edge of your hand, and then rotate the hand towards the strings and strum again. The pressure of the hand against the strings will dampen the volume and sustain – this is known as 'palm muting'. Notice how this is very different from the normal sound of strummed open strings. Now try this again with an E minor chord.

String damping, using 'palm muting': the edge of the strumming hand rests against the strings next to the bridge; the hand stays in position when you strum, to mute the strings.

When you use string damping it's not necessary
to always strum all the strings of the chord; often –
particularly in rock styles – it's better just to strum
the bass string and a couple of others. Vary the
amount of pressure with which the side of the hand
rests on the strings: if you press too hard the notes
will just become dead thuds, but if you press too
lightly the strings will start to ring and sustain again.
Be aware that it's all too easy at first to pull the
damping hand away from the strings as you begin

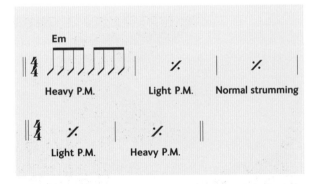

Palm muting: Measure 1: press firmly against the strings.
Measure 2: lighten the pressure. Measure 3: release
damping hand. Measure 4: re-apply damping hand,
increasing pressure in the final measure.

to strum, so losing the muting effect. Although it may take a while to gain control of this technique, and to strike the right balance of pressure and release, it's well worth the effort as string damping is an essential tool that will broaden your technique.

Palm muting can also be used in lead playing, resulting in a very staccato sound (with all the notes short and detached). This technique is often used in funk music.

183

Fretting-hand Damping

You can also mute the strings by slightly relaxing the pressure on the strings that you are fretting; the fingers still touch the strings, but do not press them all the way down to the fretboard. This technique can be used after a note has been picked to achieve a staccato effect, or after a chord has been strummed to achieve a chord 'chop'.

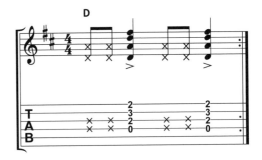

Fretting-hand damping: the fretting hand begins by touching, rather than pressing, the strings. This causes the notes to be muted. On the accented beats, the notes of the chord are fretted normally so that the chord sounds clearly when strummed strongly.

The technique can also be used to bring out accents, by damping the fretting hand continuously while the strumming hand plays a rhythm – the fretting hand only pressing the chord intermittently, so that it sounds only on the beats to be accented.

You'll have to look carefully but note the difference in pressure between the photos above and below.

Slurs

Slurring is a method that not only enables you to play much faster than with normal picking, but also provides a much smoother (legato) sound. There are two slurring techniques: 'hammering-on' and 'pulling-off'.

Pull-offs

When moving from one note to a lower note on the same string you may not want to pick the string again. By removing your finger from the higher note with a slight pulling motion, you essentially pluck that string with your fretting hand, thus creating a pull-off.

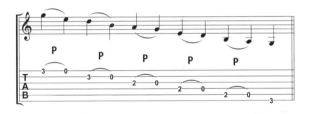

G pentatonic major scale played descending using pull-offs. The curved slur line and P sign indicate which notes should be pulled-off.

Hammer-ons and pull-offs of two fretted notes are limited by the distance you can stretch the fingers of your fretting hand, but you can also hammer-on from (or pull-off to) open strings, creating whatever intervals sound good to you.

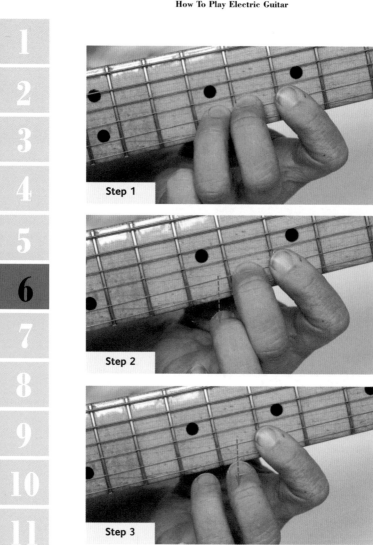

Step 1

Step 2

Step 3

The pull-off technique: a pull-off with two fingers.

Hammer-ons

When moving from one note to a higher note on the same string it's not always necessary to pick the string again. By forcefully bringing down your finger on to the new fret while the previous note is sounding you create a hammer-on. You may need to pick the first note a little harder than other picked notes, as its vibrations will need to carry over to the hammered-on note. The notes may sound more even on an electric guitar because of natural or added sustain, but acoustic guitarists use hammer-ons just as frequently.

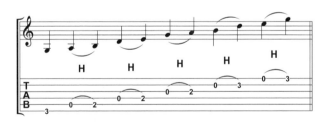

G pentatonic major scale played ascending using hammer-ons. The curved slur line and the H sign indicate which notes should be hammered-on.

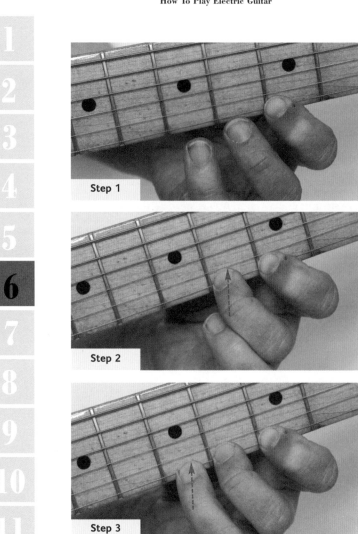

Step 1

Step 2

Step 3

A hammer-on: each finger hammers down in quick succession.

Combining Hammer-ons

and Pull-offs

Once you've mastered the basic techniques described above, try the slurring exercises below, which combine both hammer-ons and pull-offs.

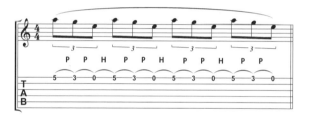

Combination slur, Exercise 1: Two pull-offs lead to an open string, then hammer back on and start again, so that only the very first note is picked.

Combination slur, Exercise 2: Use a hammer-on, then a pull-off, on each note of the A natural minor scale descending along the fifth string – picking only the first of each three notes.

Trill

If you repeatedly hammer-on and pull-off between the same two notes it is known as a 'trill'. This is a technique favoured by many rock guitarists, from Jimi Hendrix to Steve Vai.

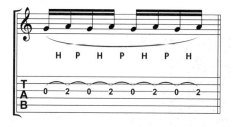

A trill: alternately hammering-on and pulling-off rapidly between the notes G and A.

Tip

On an electric guitar slurring is much easier if your guitar is adjusted to have a low action. Using a compressor (usually with a distortion effect) will help your slurs sound uniform and even.

Slides

Sliding from one note or chord to another is a great way of creating a seamless legato sound that can make your playing sound relaxed and effortless. The technique also provides an easy way of adding passing notes to make your playing unique and inventive.

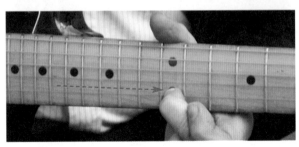

The slide technique: a slide from a high note to a low note using heavy sustain.

Slide Technique

To slide a note means to fret it and then, while maintaining the fretting pressure, to move the finger to another fret on the same string without picking the note again. The second note is sounded only because of the continued pressure of the fretting hand.

In a standard slide you only hear the first and last notes. However, you can also play a 'glissando' type of slide, in which all the intervening notes are also sounded.

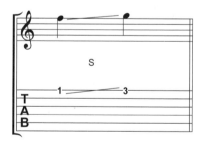

Slide: pick the F note then, using the force of the fretting finger alone, sound the G note by quickly sliding the first finger along the E string.

Controlling the amount of grip with the fretting hand is the secret to good sliding. You should try to ensure that the thumb at the back of the guitar neck relaxes its grip when you are in the process of sliding a note up or down. This doesn't mean that the thumb needs to be released totally, but simply that it shouldn't be squeezing tightly against the back of the guitar neck.

However, just as your hand reaches the note that you want to slide into, the thumb should squeeze the neck slightly harder to act as a brake, preventing your fingers sliding beyond the destination fret.

Glissando slide: pick the C note then, using the force of the fretting finger, slide along the B string up to the E note, allowing the notes in between to sound.

Sliding Chords

The guitar is one of the few instruments on which you can slide chords up and down, changing their pitch easily and smoothly; the technique creates a fluidity and smoothness of sound that piano players can only dream of! Because slides are so natural to the guitar they form a core component of any good rhythm-guitarist's technique. Slides are used by guitarists in nearly all musical styles, from metal and blues to country and ska.

When sliding chords it's important to ensure that the chord shape is maintained, so that one finger doesn't end up a fret ahead of the rest! The trick is to achieve a neutral balance whereby the chord shape is kept under control, yet at the same time the fingers are relaxed enough to slide up or down the fingerboard.

Playing fifth 'power chords', where only two notes are fretted, is the ideal introduction to sliding chords.

197

Playing power chords with a copious amount of distortion is the easiest way to begin chord sliding; the distortion will provide sustain, which will encourage you not to grip too hard when sliding the chords. Using ascending slides (raising the pitch of a chord) is easier at first – the volume tends to disappear quite quickly with descending slides.

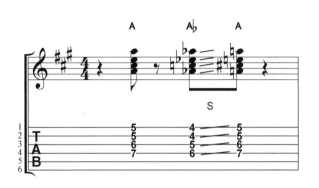

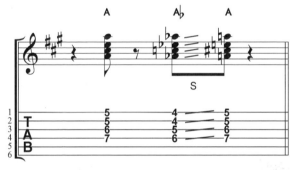

ABOVE: Example of using slides with major chords. Note that the first finger frets the top two strings. You'll need to keep a strong pressure with the fretting finger in order to maintain volume.

OPPOSITE: Example of using slides with power chords. Start with an ascending slide, from two frets below the destination chord, followed by a double slide (sliding down and then back up one fret).

Vibrato

By repeatedly varying the pitch of a note very slightly you can achieve an effect known as 'vibrato'. This is used on most string instruments, but it is particularly useful on electric guitar because of the instrument's potentially long sustain – especially if an overdriven sound is used.

Using vibrato can turn a plain solo into something that sounds really classy. Vibrato can help you make the most of the guitar's sustain, and make your playing more expressive.

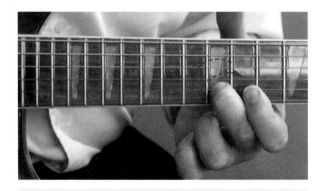

One of the main vibrato techniques.

Vibrato is often confused with string bending (see pages 206–11), but in fact they are two completely different techniques (although the two are sometimes played together within a lick). The main difference between the two techniques is that string bending involves substantially changing the pitch of a note (usually by a half step or more), whereas vibrato is more subtle, with the note being only 'wavered' with a very small variation in pitch (always returning to, and alternating with, the original pitch).

Vibrato Types

There are **three main types** of vibrato.

1. **Horizontal vibrato:** rock the fretting hand from side to side, along the direction of the string. Keep the fretting finger in contact with the string, but release the pressure of the thumb on the back of the neck. This type of vibrato will give you

increased sustain with just the tiniest variation in pitch. You can rock the hand either slowly or quickly, and for as short or long a time as you wish, depending upon the sound you want to achieve. Classic exponents of this type of vibrato include Mike Oldfield, Mark Knopfler, Dominic Miller, Carlos Santana and John Williams.

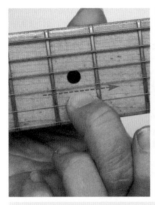 

Horizontal vibrato showing motion of finger

2. **Wrist vibrato**: while the first finger frets a note, the pitch can be wavered by rotating the wrist away from the fingerboard and back again repeatedly. This is one of the best-sounding vibratos, and can result in a sweet, singing tone.

Wrist vibrato showing motion of finger

However, it can only be used on notes that are fretted by the first finger. The undisputed master of this technique is blues legend B.B. King. Modestly he states: 'I won't say I invented it, but they weren't doing it before I started.' This style of vibrato has been an everyday tool of blues and rock guitar players. B.B. King tends to keep his thumb pressed on the back of the neck to get a fast but short pitch-range, 'stinger' vibrato. Other players, such as Eric Clapton, prefer to release the thumb in order to achieve a slower, wider-ranging vibrato.

3. **Vertical vibrato**: while fretting a note, repeatedly waggle the tip of the fretting finger to move the string up and down slightly. You don't need to move it too far and you should always make sure that you return the string to its starting position. This type of vibrato is ideal for adding to a string bend. Once a note is bent you can add vibrato to it to add a subtle enhancement to the bend and add sustain.

Peter Green and Paul Kossoff were two of the classic exponents of this technique. Other guitarists employed their own variations on the technique: Buddy Guy and Ritchie Blackmore,

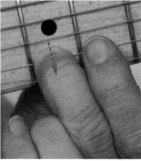

Vertical vibrato showing motion of finger

for example, often prefer to use a very fast 'stinging' vibrato after a bend, while Gary Moore and Yngwie Malmsteen tend to use wider, more extreme vibrato.

Vibrato Notation

In music notation, vibrato is indicated by a horizontal wavy line. Sometimes the abbreviation 'vib.' is also written. Occasionally, the word 'wide' might be written to indicate wide vibrato, but generally the type of vibrato used is left to the discretion of the performer.

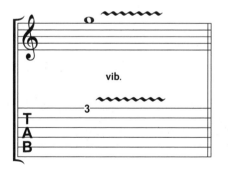

String Bends

String bending is one of the most essential techniques for any electric guitarist. Nearly every rock or blues guitarist since the Fifties has used string bending as a way of expressing emotion through their playing. Acoustic guitarists use bends too, but electronic instruments and effects have greatly extended the range of string-bending possibilities.

String bending is the perfect vehicle for adding emotion, expression and individuality to your lead

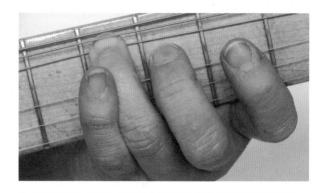

On an electric guitar, a subtle bend can add a fluid texture to a melody, especially when combined with sustain.

playing. By carefully pushing a string upwards while fretting it, you can alter the pitch of the note that you are playing without needing to move to another fret. Classic exponents include Jimi Hendrix, Eric Clapton, B.B. King, David Gilmour and Ritchie Blackmore, but listen to any guitar-based band today and you'll still hear the technique in regular use in almost every solo.

Bending Technique

In theory, you can bend any note in any scale as long as you bend it up to reach another note in that scale. In practice, most bends will be restricted to the next note in the scale – i.e. a half step (the equivalent of one fret) or a whole step (the equivalent of two frets) higher than the fretted note. You can use any finger to bend a note but, so as not to move out of position and lose fluency, it's best to use the finger that you would normally use to fret the note within the scale.

207

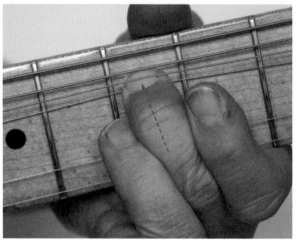

Bending technique: three-string and single-string bends.
(Use two or three fingers to strengthen the control.)

If you're executing the bend with the third or fourth finger, it's really important that you use the remaining fingers on the same string to give you added strength when bending. Ignoring this advice will mean that your bends won't go high enough to be in tune, or if they do, then you could end up straining your finger.

Bending in Tune

There are several ways to begin mastering string bends. If you're a good singer you can practise making the string bend until its pitch matches the note you're singing. Another method is to repeatedly pick the string while bending it up very slowly so that you can hear the note gradually bend into tune. The essential thing is to listen as you bend, because not much sounds worse than badly out-of-tune string bending!

It's important to practise string bends in a range of keys, because the amount of pressure that you need

209

will vary greatly depending upon your position on the fingerboard. For instance, bending a note on the third fret of the third sting will be much harder than bending on the 12th fret on the same string.

Once you feel confident that you are able to bend a note in tune, try playing through these examples, which start with third-finger half-step bends, before progressing to third- and fourth-finger whole-step bends.

Third-finger half-step bend: using the A blues scale, the D note on the G string is bent up a half step to E♭, then let down to D, using the third finger.

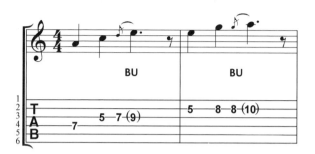

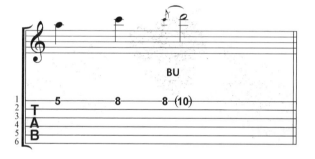

Third- and fourth-finger whole-step bend: using the A pentatonic minor scale, all the bent notes are raised up a whole step. Bend each note slowly until it's in tune, and then hold it there. Use the fourth finger to bend the notes on the second and first string; when doing so, make sure that the second and third fingers are also on the string to give extra strength and support to the fourth finger.

Plectrum Technique

Most electric guitarists want to play fast, and developing great speed starts with having proper control over your plectrum. If you start by holding the plectrum the wrong way you can develop habits that will make it hard to become a fast and accurate player.

Gripping the Plectrum

The best method is to grip the plectrum between the thumb and index finger. Position the plectrum so that its point is about half a centimetre (¼ of an inch) beyond the fingertip. Use only the tip of the plectrum to pick the strings or you will create a physical resistance that will slow down your playing. However,

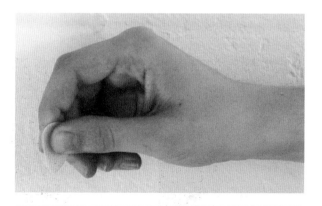

bear in mind that if you show too little plectrum you might end up missing the string altogether. Experiment until you get just the right balance. Also, be mindful of how you grip the plectrum. If you use too much pressure your hand muscles will tighten and so reduce your fluency, but if you hold it too loosely you'll keep dropping it.

Hold the plectrum so that it's in line with your fingernail. Avoid holding it at right angles to your index finger, as this will cause your wrist to lock.

How to hold your plectrum. Notice the angle and amount of plectrum tip showing.

Alternate Picking

If you want to achieve any degree of speed with
the plectrum for lead playing then it's best to use
'alternate picking' as the mainstay of your plectrum
technique. This involves alternating downstrokes
and upstrokes. Alternate picking is the most logical
and economical way of playing, since once you have
picked a string downwards, the plectrum will then
be ideally positioned to pick upwards, whereas if
you try to play two downstrokes in a row you will
need to raise the plectrum back up before you can
strike the string again.

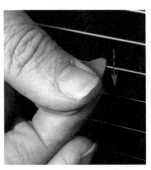 

Alternate picking can be used on any string.

When alternating down- and upstrokes, make sure that the picking action is generated by swivelling the wrist; try to avoid moving the elbow up and down as this will make your picking style much too cumbersome and will hamper your fluency. For fast lead playing, alternate picking and a relaxed wrist action are the fundamental requirements.

Picking Exercises

Begin by practising alternate picking on the open sixth string. Once you have a secure plectrum technique you can make your licks sound faster by doubling, or even quadrupling, your picking on some notes. The fretting hand may be moving quite slowly, but the lick will sound more mobile because of the activity of the picking hand. Practise this technique at first by playing scales with double and quadruple picking. A fast rock sound can be achieved by mixing fretted

C major scale, played ascending with double picking and descending with quadruple picking.

notes with an open string – while the right hand
keeps picking with alternate down- and upstrokes.

Triplet Picking

A great way of making your playing sound super-fast
is to use triplet picking patterns. Because these

216

patterns cut across the standard $\frac{4}{4}$ rhythm, they give the impression of being much faster than they really are. This repeated 'down-up-down' picking style can give a rolling or galloping effect to a piece of music. (The term 'triplet' here refers only to the three-part picking action; the rhythm doesn't have to be a triplet in the traditional musical sense.)

Use a 'down-up-down' picking pattern for each triplet.

217

Effects

The beauty of playing an electric guitar
is that you can alter or colour its sound
with a multitude of effects. These range
from dynamic effects, such as
compression, and alteration of tone,
such as distortion, to changing the pitch
and frequency using chorus effects and
flanging and phasing. Delay and reverb
are effective time-based effects, and
volume and wah-wah pedals give you
impressive tonal effects.

Compression

To understand the use of compressors, it helps to understand the difference between distortion and sustain. Distortion is a quality of sound; sustain refers to how long the note, clean or distorted, remains audible. Compression can be used to increase 'apparent' sustain without any distortion. Think of a compressor as an automatic volume pedal; first, the compressor restricts the guitar signal to a pre-set level. Then, as the string vibration slows and the guitar volume drops, an amplifier in the compressor raises it back to the same level as the initial attack.

Pedal compressors are used to control volume levels and reduce dynamic range.

What Does it Sound Like?

On a guitar, a compressor's effect is easy to hear, because a guitar, like a piano, has a wide 'dynamic range' (the difference between soft notes and loud notes). A heavily compressed guitar signal sounds 'squeezed', because its normal dynamic range has been limited. Yet this compression helps a guitar sound 'pop out' in a mix, and the sustain created adds warmth to distortion effects.

Compressor Applications

1. For clean rhythms, or country 'chicken picking', you can create a squeezing effect by setting a quick attack.

2. The added sustained volume helps to make chorusing and flanging effects considerably more dramatic.

3. It can provide controlled feedback with minimal distortion and volume.

Distortion

Distortion is the sound of rock guitar, created originally, and still optimally, by sending a signal that is 'too hot' into an amplifier not designed to take it. This is called overdriving the amp. Another way of getting a distorted guitar tone is with an effects unit or 'stomp box' pedal. Different pedals may be labelled with terms like distortion, overdrive or fuzz, which describe different levels of distorted sound.

Getting the Right Effect

Modern stompboxes create a more natural-sounding distortion. Some pedals use an actual tube, while others use increasingly sophisticated chips to offer the feel and sound of an overdriven amp. Most distortion

An overdrive pedal maintains the character of the original signal.

222

1

2

3

4

5

6

7

8

9

10

11

12

devices come with controls marked 'distortion', 'drive' or 'gain'; 'level' or 'volume'; and 'tone'.

To get the most out of your distorted sound, remember that the level of the input signal will affect the distorted sound. For example, single-coil pickups will create a sound different from that generated by higher-powered humbucking pickups plugged into the same pedal. A Strat, therefore, will need a higher dose of distortion than a Les Paul to achieve a similar effect. Too much distortion, however, can make your notes indistinct, especially if you are playing fast. If your amplifier is already slightly distorted when your guitar volume is fully up, adding just a little gain on the pedal will make it sing.

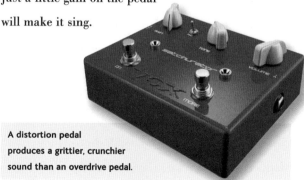

A distortion pedal produces a grittier, crunchier sound than an overdrive pedal.

Chorus

To acheive the big sound and chiming characteristics
of a 12-string guitar, you'll need a chorus effect.
It is the delay of the pick hitting one of the doubled
strings after the other, and the slight tuning
variations, that give a 12-string its distinctive sound.
The chorus pedal emulates this effect and uses delay
and pitch-shifting to achieve its end.

How Does it Work?

A chorus device delays the original signal by
approximately 20 milliseconds, varying the delay
by plus or minus about five milliseconds to create
a pitch shift. A chorus mixes the sound caused by
the delay fluctuation with the original signal, thus
emulating the effect of twice as many strings being
played slightly out of time and tune. Chorus pedals
are provided with rate and depth controls. The
depth control increases the amount of pitch

224

fluctuation, while the rate knob determines how quickly it fluctuates. Some pedals include a blend or level control that allows you to mix the amount of affected signal with the original 'dry' signal. This is handy for controlling the chorus effect, which can be undesirable on solos. Sometimes a feedback control is included to send the delayed signal back, delaying it again for a more intense effect.

A chorus pedal works by mixing a delayed signal with the original sound, usually outputting a stereo signal to emphasize the effect.

Flanging & Phasing

Supposedly the term flanging was created when an engineer placed a thumb on a recording-tape reel, or 'flange', as they are known in the UK, and liked the whooshing sound that it produced.

That effect is simulated in flanger devices by sweeping a short delay (about five to 10 milliseconds) over a wide range (from one to 10, or two to 20 milliseconds) with a certain amount of feedback, or recycling of the delay.

Phaser vs. Flanger

Flangers are confused with phasers (phase shifters) due to the similar sweeping sound. Phase shifters use an even shorter delay and almost

A phaser has a characteristic swirling sound that can be varied with a speed control to provide colour to a rhythm-guitar part or increased to produce a bubbling effect.

226

no feedback, continually sweeping the dry and delayed signals in and out of phase. A phase shifter produces a more subtle, musical effect than a flanger with its more edgy, metallic sound.

A Distinctive Sound

As well as speed or rate controls, flangers often have an added control marked 'feedback' or 'regeneration'. This recycles the delay back through itself and increases the 'metallic' sound of the effect. A flanger set for a medium rate, lower depth and minimal feedback can mimic a mild chorus effect. A slow sweep with more intense depth and feedback settings will get closer to the Hendrix or Van Halen sound.

As well as producing a whooshing sound, the flanger also produces a metallic warbling reminiscent of sci-fi movie ray guns.

Delay

As the spatial environment in which you play your guitar may not always be ideal, engineers invented effects such as delay and reverb that help to restore a natural room ambience. These effects allow the guitar to sound like it is being played in a huge empty hall, even in a small club or basement studio.

Tape Delay

Les Paul was one of the first to discover tape delay. Running a signal into a reel-to-reel tape recorder, he recorded it on the machine's 'record' head and played it back as it passed over the 'playback' head milliseconds later. Combining the two signals created a delay effect. Recycling the delayed signal created additional repeats. The discovery of the tape-delay effect in the studio created demand for a unit that could recreate the effect live. Thus the Echoplex, a portable tape echo, was born. Alternatives quickly appeared in the form of analogue and digital delays.

Analogue Delay

In analogue delays the sound quality of the echoes diminishes significantly as the delay times and number of repeats increase. After about a half-second of delay, analogue delay units add significant noise and unpleasant distortion. Still, many guitarists value analogue delays for their warmth, and the fact that the degradation of the signal with each repeat avoids conflict with the dry signal, sounding more natural to some guitarists.

Analogue delays appeared in the 1970s and are the link between tape and digital delays.

Digital Delay

Digital technology solved some of the problems inherent in analogue delays. While analogue delays repeat the signal electronically, digital delays sample the original signal, turning it into digital code. The code is then processed and translated back into a signal again before sending it to the output. Since the encoded signal is less subject to degradation, it allows for longer delays with less distortion.

Using Delay

Delays can be used for ambience, for doubling, for creating rhythmic patterns and for many other effects. Most delays have three controls. One is 'delay length'; this can be called delay 'time', 'effect', 'range' or simply 'delay'. Another control affects the number of repeats, from a single repetition of the signal to

Digital delays sample the guitar's sound and play it back after a defined period.

'runaway' feedback; this knob can be called 'feedback', 'regen' (regeneration) or repeat. The third controls the amount of effect added to the original or 'dry' signal. This may be called 'mix', 'blend' or 'level'. Many delays also have a dry output and an effect output, which lets you send them to separate channels or amps and create your own mix of the two signals.

Artificial Ambience

Increasing the delay time increases the apparent room size, but remember to decrease the number of repeats as you increase the length of the delay unless you want to sound like you are playing in a cave.

Digital delays work well for a doubling effect. For this you need the delay to be as clean as possible since it will be mixed equally, or almost equally, with the original. The delay should be long enough to fatten the sound, but short enough so that it is not a rhythmic pattern. Use a single repeat or it will start to sound like reverb.

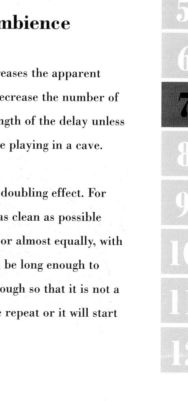

Rhythmic Delays & Looping

Digital delays let you set up rhythmic repeat patterns. These can produce uniformly 'retro' or 'spacey' sounds, or result in polyrhythmic patterns. Looping delays can provide a single guitarist with extra parts, or can create highly textured, atmospheric pads.

Looping Effects

Digital delays with longer delay times (two seconds or more) allow you to create 'looping' effects by playing along with yourself, in the manner of Robert Fripp, Bill Frisell

A looping device can add texture to your playing.

232

and others. One way to do this is to set a very long delay time, with an even mix and the feedback high. This way, as old patterns fade, you can overlay new ones. Another way is to use the hold button (present on almost all digital delays) to lock in what you have played up to that point and then improvise over the repeats. Some delays include specific 'looping' functions, and some devices are meant for looping alone.

Time-based Delays

To create rhythmic delays you need to understand the relationship between tempo, in beats-per-minute (BPM), and delay time, in milliseconds (ms). For example, at 120 BPM (two beats per second) one beat equals 500 ms. A sixteenth-note delay is one-quarter of this, or 125 ms. Faster tempos mean shorter delay times; slower tempos mean longer delay times.

Reverb

Reverb plays a major role in defining a guitarist's sound. Even a lack of reverb makes a statement about the kind of music you are making. In general, it is an effect that moves the sound further away from the listener the more it is applied.

Spring Reverb

An early type of mechanical reverb was the spring reverb. Found in many guitar amplifiers, it employs a transducer to convert the signal from electrical energy to mechanical energy, then sends it down a spring or springs to another transducer, where it is converted back to electrical energy. The time it takes to travel the length of the spring adds delay.

The spring reverb's sound is created from the physical reverberations of a physical spring.

The spring degrades the frequency response in a more uneven manner than analogue or digital delays, creating a more natural effect. More springs means a more natural effect, and longer springs create longer delays.

Digital Reverb

Digital reverbs can simulate virtually any size and type of room, and place the sound anywhere in it. Similarly to digital delays, digital reverbs take the signal and convert it to digital code, then add delays and frequency changes to simulate the desired room size and to place the sound in the desired location within it.

As well as simulating the sound of different room spaces, digital reverb can also mimic the sound of artificial reverb devices, such as reverb plates and chambers used in studios.

Volume &
Wah-wah Pedals

By placing volume and tone controls, like those on your guitar, into pedals, manufacturers transformed those tools into creative effects.

Volume Pedal

The volume pedal has myriad uses. At its most basic, it allows you to adjust your volume without interrupting play, maintaining the proper mix with the band.

Many guitarists were inspired to explore volume pedals by pedal-steel players, who constantly manipulate one while playing. You will find that your pedal-steel licks sound more authentic if you swell into them with a pedal. You can also create lush pads with a volume pedal and

The extremely versatile volume pedal.

236

a delay: add distortion and play single low notes for a cello effect, or higher ones for a violin sound.

Wah-wah

Unlike a guitar's tone control, a wah-wah pedal has active circuitry that boosts the highs at one end and the lows at the other. Often rocked in time for rhythmic effect, it can also be used for expressive tonal effects. The riff on the Dire Straits' hit 'Money For Nothing' (1984) is the sound of a partially backed-off wah-wah pedal. Accenting the treble on bent notes gives a distinct vocal effect, while slow sweeping through the range as you play a rhythmic part can emulate a synthesizer filter.

Getting Pedal-steel Effects

1. Plug your guitar into a volume pedal.
2. Plug the pedal into your amplifier.
3. Play a chord and gradually increase the volume with the pedal from zero to full.
4. If your guitar has a vibrato arm, gently rock it.
5. Add a long delay for a richer effect.

Combining Effects

Once you understand the workings of individual
effects you will want to combine them to create
sounds you have heard, or to make some new sounds.
Effects can be combined in many ways. Pedals can be
attached to a pedalboard, or placed in a rack pedal
drawer and triggered remotely along with rack
devices. Or you may want to use one of the many
multi-effects units available in rack or pedal form.

Multi-effects Units

Many manufacturers offer multi-effects units. These
can come in a floorboard system or a rack unit that
requires a separate controller, usually using MIDI, a
protocol that allows devices to communicate with one
another. The advantage
of a multi-effects unit

A multi-effects unit can
be useful if you don't
have a lot of space.

is that you can program it to switch numerous effects on and off simultaneously. Thus, with one motion you could conceivably turn your distortion and delay on and your chorus and compressor off. The disadvantage is that modifying the settings of the effects is not as easy as bending down and turning a knob on a pedal.

A common compromise is a rack with a drawer for pedals and a switcher that brings the pedals in and out of the signal path in pre-set combinations.

Pedals on a Board

No matter which pedals you use, where you place them in the 'signal chain' will determine your final sound. Dynamics processors, like compressors, should do their work earlier while a volume pedal would be one of the last devices in the chain. Here is a possible sequence of effects that would work well in most cases:

1. Compressor
2. Tuner
3. Fuzz
4. Wah-wah
5. Distortion/overdrive

6. Chorus/flanger/tremolo
7. Volume
8. Delay
9. Reverb

239

8

More Techniques

The techniques explained here will add
range and variety to your playing.
Using a bottleneck is a great way to
acheive a smooth slide. Arpeggios,
octaves and harmonics will all add
interest and power to your sound.
Finally, employing alternative tunings
will enable you to create a unique
sound on your guitar.

1
2
3
4
5
6
7
8
9
10
11
12

Bottleneck or Slide Guitar

A bottleneck (also known as a 'slide') is a tubular device that can be used instead of the fingers for sounding notes. Using a bottleneck is a great technique for musical styles such as blues, country and rock music when you want to slide between notes and achieve smooth glissandos. Originally, the bottleneck guitar sound was created by running a glass neck from a bottle along the strings. Early blues players sometimes used other objects, such as whiskey glasses and knives.

Nowadays guitarists can benefit from specially manufactured metal, glass or plastic tubes. The metal versions are technically known as 'slides', although in practice the terms 'slide' and 'bottleneck' are often interchanged. Glass bottlenecks give a more rounded tone, but they create less sustain than the metal versions.

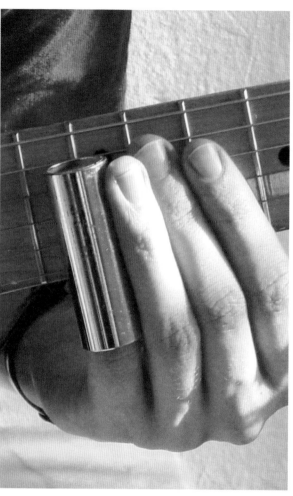

When using a bottleneck, the centre of the tube must rest over the centre of the fret, rather than just behind it.

Using the Bottleneck

Most players tend to place the bottleneck on the
third or fourth finger: using the fourth finger enables
the third finger to remain free for normal fretting,
but this is dependent upon the fourth finger being
large enough to support the bottleneck.

To reach the correct pitch, the middle of the
bottleneck should be held directly over the fret,

Bottleneck guitar lick in standard tuning. A slide
movement is made on the second string from two frets
below up to a two-note chord. Be sure to mute unused
strings with either the side of the picking hand or with
the lower fingers of the bottleneck hand.

rather than behind it as when fretting a note. The bottleneck only needs to touch the strings; you should not try to press against the frets with the bottleneck as this will cause fretbuzz and result in the notes being out of tune.

Bottleneck is usually played using some vibrato. This is achieved by moving the bottleneck slightly backwards and forwards along the strings above the target fret.

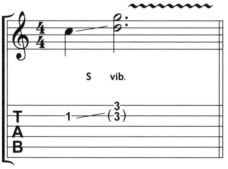

Vibrato is essential for any bottleneck guitarist. It can be achieved by keeping the bottleneck vertical and moving slightly from left to right above the fret, but always returning to the correct pitch.

Basic Arpeggios

Learning arpeggios is a good way of developing a comprehensive knowledge of the guitar fingerboard. But arpeggios aren't just technical exercises – they're great for soloing and can make your lead playing more melodic by emphasizing the harmonic structure of the underlying chord progression.

Constructing Arpeggios

An arpeggio is simply the notes of a chord played individually. Standard major and minor chords, and therefore their arpeggios, contain only three different notes. For example, if you look closely at the open position C major chord you'll notice that although you're playing five strings, there are in fact only three different notes (C E G) in the chord. If you play these notes consecutively, rather than strum them simultaneously, then you've created a C major arpeggio.

C major chord   C major arpeggio.

When you're first learning arpeggios it's helpful to practise them in the set order (1st, 3rd, 5th, 8th), but once you know them you can improvise freely by swapping the notes around, or repeating some, to make up an interesting lick or riff, just as you would when improvising with a scale.

The really useful thing is that, because the C major arpeggio contains exactly the same notes as the C major chord, whatever notes you play from the C major arpeggio when improvising will always be totally in tune with a C major chordal accompaniment.

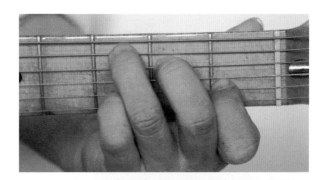

Step 1. Thumb

Step 2. First finger

ABOVE TOP: C major fingerboard position.

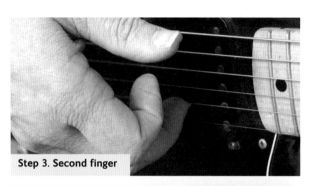

Step 3. Second finger

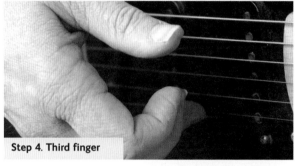

Step 4. Third finger

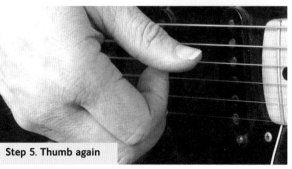

Step 5. Thumb again

LEFT and ABOVE: Playing a C major arpeggio.

1
2
3
4
5
6
7
8
9
10
11
12

Major and Minor Arpeggios

Each basic major or minor arpeggio will only contain three notes; you can work out which notes these are by analyzing the relevant chord shape. A major arpeggio always contains the first, third and fifth notes of the major scale with the same starting note (for example, C E G are the 1st, 3rd and 5th notes of the C major scale and so form the C major arpeggio).

To work out minor arpeggios flatten the third note of the major arpeggio by a half step (e.g. C minor arpeggio contains the notes C E♭ G).

Aim to acquire knowledge of all major and minor arpeggios in as many fingerboard positions as possible. Here are some fingerboard positions for C major and C minor arpeggios. They can be transposed to other pitches by moving them up or down the fingerboard.

250

First C major arpeggio pattern.

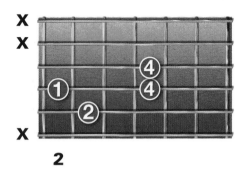

Second C major arpeggio pattern.

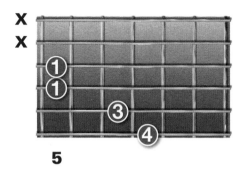

5

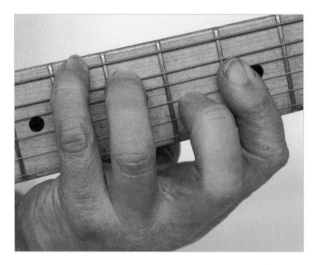

Third C major arpeggio pattern.

First C minor arpeggio pattern.

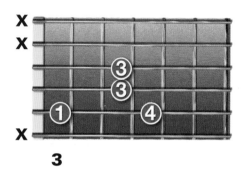

3

Second C minor arpeggio pattern.

Using Arpeggios

You can use arpeggios for riffs and lead playing. When you use a scale for a lead solo you'll notice that some notes sound more resolved against certain chords than other notes. This problem disappears when you use arpeggios; because the notes of each arpeggio are taken from the chord they will all sound completely 'in tune' – providing you're playing the right arpeggio for each chord. If you've only used scales before, this takes a little getting used to as you'll need to change arpeggio every time there is a chord change.

In a normal playing situation guitarists rarely use arpeggios throughout a whole solo, as this approach

Tip

For a second guitar an arpeggio can add great colour to a song, playing the same chord as a first guitar, but using a differnet position or inversion.

can tend to sound almost too 'in tune'. Instead, arpeggios are used to add colour over just a couple of chords, and the normal key scale is used for the majority of the solo.

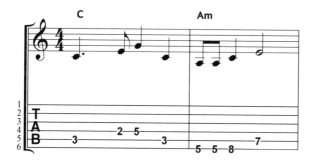

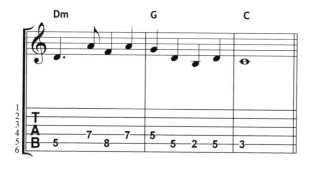

Lead line using notes only from the arpeggios of each chord.

Octaves

Octave playing is an instant way of giving more power and solidity to your playing, and because of this it is a technique that is often used by jazz and rock musicians alike. Learning octaves is also one of the quickest ways of getting to know all the notes on the fretboard.

Playing octaves involves playing two of the same notes together (e.g. C and C), but with one of those notes at a higher pitch (i.e. an octave above). The fact that the two notes are the same is what gives octave playing its powerful sound and avoids the excessive sweetness that is often associated with other pairings of notes.

Bass Octaves

There are various ways in which octaves can be played, but for notes on the bass strings by far the most common way is to add a note two frets and two strings higher. For example, if your original note is A on the fifth fret of the sixth string, then the octave A will be on the seventh fret of the fourth string. Similarly, if your original note is D on the fifth fret of the fifth string, then the octave D will be on the seventh fret of the third string. This system, of finding the octave two frets and two strings higher than the original note, will work for all notes on the sixth and fifth strings. The lower note should be played with the first finger, while the octave can be fretted with either the third or the fourth finger.

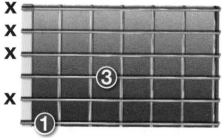

Octave shape based upon the 6th string.

Octave shape based upon the 5th string.

The most important technique when playing bass octaves is to ensure that the string between the lower note and the octave is totally muted. This should be done by allowing the first finger to lie across it lightly – not fretting the string but just deadening it. You should also be careful not to strum the strings above the octave note, and as a precaution it's a good idea to mute them by allowing the octave-fretting finger to lightly lie across them.

RIGHT: A bass octave slide can be achieved by moving your hand up or down two frets along one string.

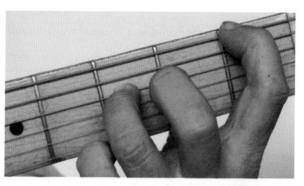

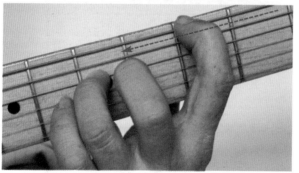

Treble Octaves

The easiest way of playing octaves on the treble
strings is to use a similar approach to that described
above, but with the octave note requiring a further
one-fret stretch. For the fourth and third strings the

octave notes can be found by playing three frets and two strings higher. For example, if your original note is G on the fifth fret of the fourth string then the octave G will be on the eighth fret of the second string.

Octave shape based upon the 4th (or D) string.

Octave shape based upon the 3rd or (G) string.

This system of finding the octave three frets and two strings higher than the original note will work for all notes on the fourth and third strings.

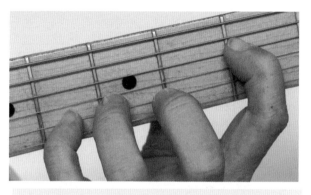

ABOVE: A treble octave based upon the 4th (or D) string.

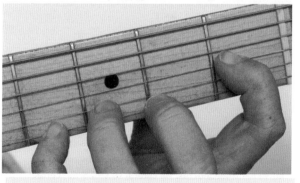

A treble octave based upon the 3rd (or G) string.

Sixth string octave riff. Notice how much stronger this riff sounds when it is played the second time with the octave note added.

Sixth and fifth string octaves. Using octaves starting from two strings can minimize the amount of fingerboard movement needed. Just be careful to strum the correct strings and make sure that unwanted strings between the fretted notes are fully muted.

Playing Octaves

Once you're familiar with the octave shapes try to play through the examples of octave use given opposite.

Fingerboard Knowledge

Once you're familiar with the octave shapes you can use them to learn the notes all across the fingerboard. For example, assuming that you can memorize the notes on the sixth string you can then use your octave shape to work out instantly where the same notes will appear on the fourth string.

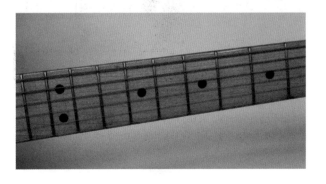

Harmonics

Harmonics can add interesting bell-like chimes to your guitar playing, and are a useful way of sustaining notes. Harmonics are also a great way of adding an extended pitch range to your playing by enabling you to play notes that are much higher than the pitch you can normally reach on the fingerboard.

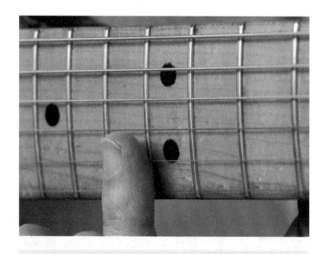

Harmonics enable notes higher than those fretted to be played. Note how lightly the finger touches the string.

Natural Harmonics

There are various forms of harmonics that can be played on the guitar, but natural harmonics are the easiest to learn at first. Natural harmonics occur on all strings on frets 12, seven and five (and 12 frets up from these). Natural harmonics also occur on frets nine and four, although making these ring clearly is a bit harder.

The best way to start playing natural harmonics is to pick the low E string and then touch that string right

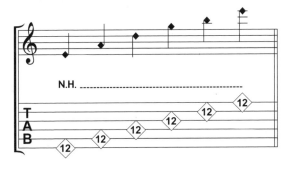

Natural harmonics at the 12th fret.

267

above the 12th fret. Don't fret the note in the normal way by pressing down onto the fingerboard; instead just lightly touch the string directly over the fretwire. The harmonics on fret 12 produce the same notes

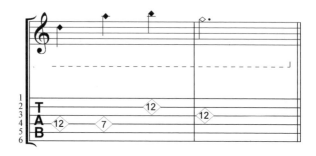

Natural harmonics have a chiming, bell-like quality.

268

(although with a different tone) as the 12th-fret fretted
notes, but harmonics at all other fingerboard positions
affect the pitch of the note produced: the harmonic

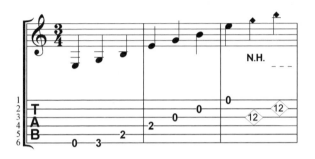

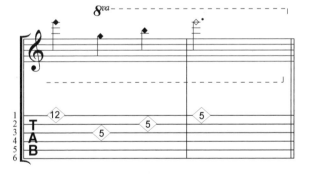

The E minor arpeggio is extended to four octaves by the
use of harmonics. Unless you have a 24-fret guitar, the last
note would be impossible without using harmonics.

notes on fret seven are an octave higher than the fretted notes; the harmonic notes on fret five are the same as the 12th fret fretted notes but an octave higher; the harmonic notes on fret four are two octaves higher than the fretted notes. Natural harmonics also occur on fret nine, and 12 frets up from the previously mentioned fret numbers (e.g. 17, 19, 24).

Other Harmonics

- **'Tapped harmonics'** (or 'touch harmonics') are played by fretting and picking a note as normal and then touching the same string 12 or seven frets higher.

- **'Artificial harmonics'** are similar to tapped harmonics, in that you touch the string 12 frets higher than the fretted note. However, in this technique, instead of picking the fretted note first, you pick the string with the third finger of the picking hand after you have positioned the first finger over the 'harmonic note'.

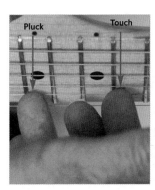

A tapped harmonic on the the second fret, showing left and right hand positions

- **'Pinched harmonics'** are often used in rock for making screeching high notes appear out of nowhere in the middle of a lick. The effect is achieved by fretting a note normally and then picking the string with the side edge of the plectrum while allowing the side of the thumb to almost immediately touch the string – so creating a harmonic. The quality and pitch of the sound that you achieve depends upon where you pick the string. Start by trying to locate the 'nodal point' – that is the equivalent of 24 frets (i.e. two octaves) higher than the note you are fretting.

1
2
3
4
5
6
7
8
9
10
11
12

Alternative Tunings

Discover a new range of beautiful chordal harmonies
by simply tuning your guitar in a different way.
If you sometimes start to feel restricted by sticking
to the same chord shapes you've played before, then
experimenting with alternative tunings is a great
way of generating some fresh sounds and ideas.

Dropped D Tuning

There are numerous ways in which a guitar can be
retuned, but the simplest and most commonly used
is 'dropped D tuning'. All you need to do is lower
the pitch of the low E string by a whole step until it
reaches the note of D (an octave lower than the open
fourth string). You can check that you've retuned
correctly by playing on the seventh fret of the sixth
string and comparing the note to the open fifth string
they should produce exactly the same pitch.

6 = **D**

Dropped D tuning.

Dropped D tuning is perfect for playing songs in the keys of D major or D minor. Having the low D bass string is almost like having your own built-in bass player – it can add great solidity and power to your sound. To make the most of this bass effect many guitarists use the low D string as a 'drone' – i.e. they repeatedly play this low D note while moving chord shapes up and down the fingerboard. Moving a simple D major shape up the fingerboard while playing a low D drone produces a very effective sound.

D Modal Tuning

Tuning the sixth, second and first strings down a whole step creates what is known as 'D modal tuning': D A D G A D. When you need to reach this tuning unaided just remember that the A, D and G strings are tuned as normal. Playing the open D string will give you the pitch for the lowered sixth

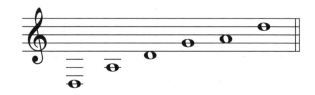

D modal tuning.

string when it is played at the 12th fret. Playing the A string at the 12th fret will give you the pitch to tune the second string down to, and playing the D string at the 12th fret will give you the pitch to tune the first string down to. Once the guitar is correctly tuned it will give you a Dsus4 chord when the open strings are all strummed, thus creating instant ambiguity and a sense of interest.

When first using this tuning, playing in the key of D will prove the easiest: by placing the first finger on the second fret of the G string you will make a nice deep-sounding D major (D5) chord.

Traditional chord shapes will not work in the same way with any altered tuning, so it's really a case of experimenting to find chord sounds that you like. The secret is to be adventurous and see what ideas you can come up with when freed from the restrictions of conventional chord shapes.

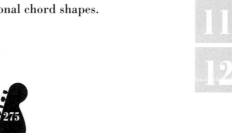

Other Tunings

If the two altered tunings described above have given you the taste for experimentation, then here are a few other tunings you can try (all shown starting with the low sixth string).

Slack key tuning – D G D G B D (the first, fifth and sixth strings are 'slackened' down a whole step to form a G major chord).

Slack key tuning.

Open E tuning – E B E G♯ B E (the third, fourth and fifth strings are tuned higher than normal to make an E major chord).

Open E tuning.

Open D tuning – D A D F♯ A D (the first, second, third and sixth strings are tuned down so that the open strings form a D major chord).

Open D tuning.

9

Playthrough

After all that hard work, we thought it would be good to put what you have learned into practice. To follow are a variety of tunes in the style of various well-known guitar players.

Rather than simply launch into the music, consider doing the following before you play:

1. Clap through the rhythm
2. Play through the rhythm on one note
3. Find the notes on your guitar
4. Play the melody (tune)
5. Gradually increase the speed until you reach the appropriate tempo.

Rory Gallagher

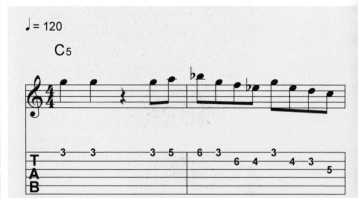

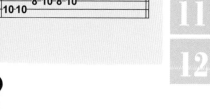

James Dean Bradfield

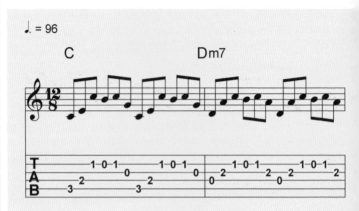

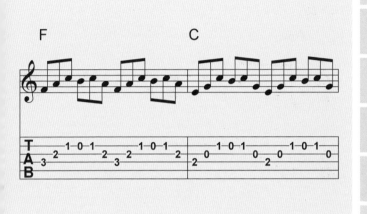

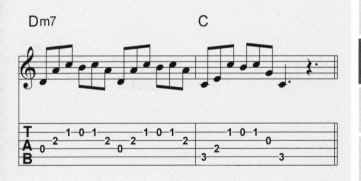

Alvin Lee

Playthrough

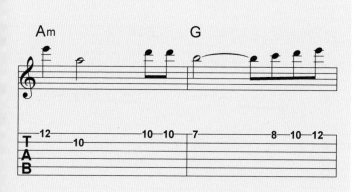

The Edge

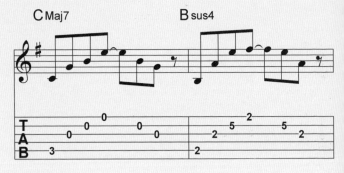

Steve Howe

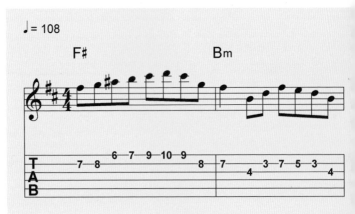

Guitar Slim

Playthrough

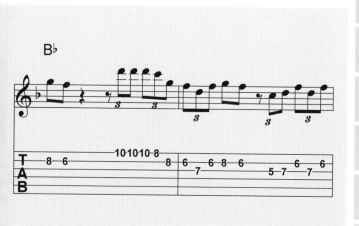

Albert King

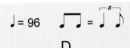

Playthrough

Peter Buck

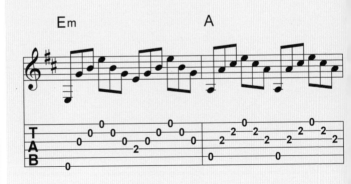

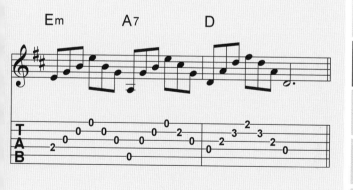

George Harrison

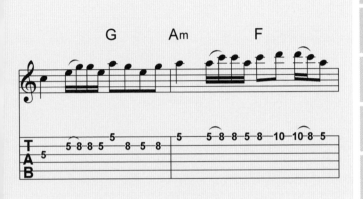

Ry Cooder

C

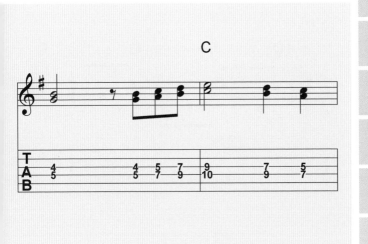

D

Roger McGuinn

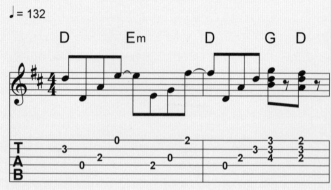

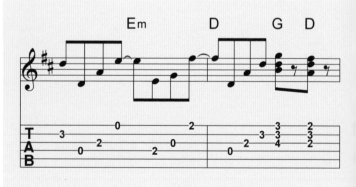

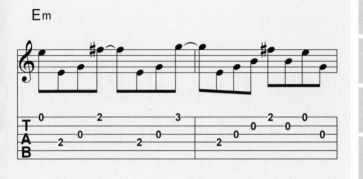

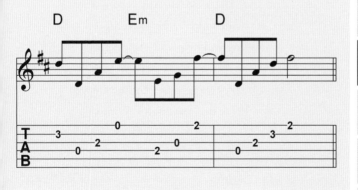

10

Chord & Scale Finder

The fretboxes and scales in this section
will help you learn the shapes of dozens
of chords and many of the most useful
scales. There are enough chords and
scales included to give you a good
grounding and help add variety to your
playing. For a more extensive look at
chords, try Flame Tree's *Guitar Chords*
and for scales, try *Scales & Modes*.

1
2
3
4
5
6
7
8
9
10
11
12

C Major

Chord Spelling
1st (C), 3rd (E), 5th (G)

C Minor

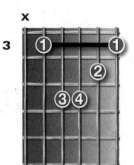

Chord Spelling
1st (C), ♭3rd (E♭), 5th (G)

C Major 7th

Chord Spelling
1st (C), 3rd (E), 5th (G),
7th (B)

C Minor 7th

Chord Spelling
1st (C), ♭3rd (E♭), 5th (G),
♭7th (B♭)

C Sus 4th

Chord Spelling
1st (C), 4th (F), 5th (G)

C Dom 7th sus4

Chord Spelling
1st (C), 4th (F), 5th (G),
♭7th (B♭)

C Major 6th

Chord Spelling
1st (C), 3rd (E), 5th (G),
6th (A)

C Minor 6th

Chord Spelling
1st (C), ♭3rd (E♭), 5th (G),
6th (A)

C♯ Major

Chord Spelling
1st (C♯), 3rd (E♯), 5th (G♯)

C♯ Minor

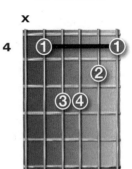

Chord Spelling
1st (C♯), ♭3rd (E), 5th (G♯)

C♯ Major 7th

Chord Spelling
1st (C♯), 3rd (E♯), 5th (G♯),
7th (B♯)

C♯ Minor 7th

Chord Spelling
1st (C♯), ♭3rd (E), 5th (G♯),
♭7th (B)

C♯ Sus 4th

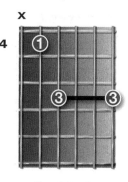

Chord Spelling
1st (C♯), 4th (F♯), 5th (G♯)

C♯ Dom 7th sus4

Chord Spelling
1st (C♯), 4th (F♯), 5th (G♯),
♭7th (B)

C♯ Major 6th

Chord Spelling
1st (C♯), 3rd (E♯), 5th (G♯),
6th (A♯)

C♯ Minor 6th

Chord Spelling
1st (C♯), ♭3rd (E), 5th (G♯),
6th (A♯)

1
2
3
4
5
6
7
8
9
10
11
12

D Major

Chord Spelling
1st (D), 3rd (F♯), 5th (A)

D Minor

Chord Spelling
1st (D), ♭3rd (F), 5th (A)

D Major 7th

Chord Spelling
1st (D), 3rd (F♯), 5th (A),
7th (C♯)

D Minor 7th

Chord Spelling
1st (D), ♭3rd (F), 5th (A),
♭7th (C)

D Sus 4th

Chord Spelling
1st (D), 4th (G), 5th (A)

D Dom 7th sus4

Chord Spelling
1st (D), 4th (G), 5th (A),
♭7th (C)

D Major 6th

Chord Spelling
1st (D), 3rd (F♯), 5th (A),
6th (B)

D Minor 6th

Chord Spelling
1st (D), ♭3rd (F), 5th (A),
6th (B)

E♭ Major

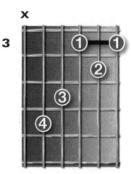

Chord Spelling
1st (E♭), 3rd (G), 5th (B♭)

E♭ Minor

Chord Spelling
1st (E♭), ♭3rd (G♭), 5th (B♭)

E♭ Major 7th

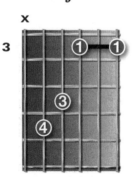

Chord Spelling
1st (E♭), 3rd (G), 5th (B♭),
7th (D)

E♭ Minor 7th

Chord Spelling
1st (E♭), ♭3rd (G♭), 5th (B♭),
♭7th (D♭)

E♭ Sus 4th

Chord Spelling
1st (E♭), 4th (A♭), 5th (B♭)

E♭ Dom 7th sus4

Chord Spelling
1st (E♭), 4th (A♭), 5th (B♭),
♭7th (D♭)

E♭ Major 6th

Chord Spelling
1st (E♭), 3rd (G), 5th (B♭),
6th (C)

E♭ Minor 6th

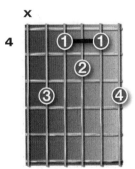

Chord Spelling
1st (E♭), ♭3rd (G♭), 5th (B♭),
6th (C)

311

E Major

Chord Spelling
1st (E), 3rd (G♯), 5th (B)

E Minor

Chord Spelling
1st (E), ♭3rd (G), 5th (B)

E Major 7th

Chord Spelling
1st (E), 3rd (G♯), 5th (B),
7th (D♯)

E Minor 7th

Chord Spelling
1st (E), ♭3rd (G), 5th (B),
♭7th (D)

E Sus 4th

Chord Spelling
1st (E), 4th (A), 5th (B)

E Dom 7th sus4

Chord Spelling
1st (E), 4th (A), 5th (B),
♭7th (D)

E Major 6th

Chord Spelling
1st (E), 3rd (G♯), 5th (B),
6th (C♯)

E Minor 6th

Chord Spelling
1st (E), ♭3rd (G), 5th (B),
6th (C♯)

F Major

Chord Spelling
1st (F), 3rd (A), 5th (C)

F Minor

Chord Spelling
1st (F), ♭3rd (A♭), 5th (C)

F Major 7th

Chord Spelling
1st (F), 3rd (A), 5th (C),
7th (E)

F Minor 7th

Chord Spelling
1st (F), ♭3rd (A♭), 5th (C),
♭7th (E♭)

314

F Sus 4th

Chord Spelling
1st (F), 4th (B♭), 5th (C)

F Dom 7th sus4

Chord Spelling
1st (F), 4th (B♭), 5th (C),
♭7th (E♭)

F Major 6th

Chord Spelling
1st (F), 3rd (A), 5th (C),
6th (D)

F Minor 6th

Chord Spelling
1st (F), ♭3rd (A♭), 5th (C),
6th (D)

F# Major

Chord Spelling
1st (F#), 3rd (A#), 5th (C#)

F# Minor

Chord Spelling
1st (F#), ♭3rd (A), 5th (C#)

F# Major 7th

Chord Spelling
1st (F#), 3rd (A#), 5th (C#),
7th (E#)

F# Minor 7th

Chord Spelling
1st (F#), ♭3rd (A), 5th (C#),
♭7th (E)

F# Sus 4th

Chord Spelling
1st (F#), 4th (B), 5th (C#)

F# Dom 7th sus4

Chord Spelling
1st (F#), 4th (B), 5th (C#),
b7th (E)

F# Major 6th

Chord Spelling
1st (F#), 3rd (A#), 5th (C#),
6th (D#)

F# Minor 6th

Chord Spelling
1st (F#), b3rd (A), 5th (C#),
6th (D#)

G Major

Chord Spelling
1st (G), 3rd (B), 5th (D)

G Minor

Chord Spelling
1st (G), ♭3rd (B♭), 5th (D)

G Major 7th

Chord Spelling
1st (G), 3rd (B), 5th (D),
7th (F♯)

G Minor 7th

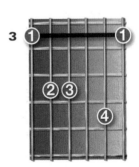

Chord Spelling
1st (G), ♭3rd (B♭), 5th (D),
♭7th (F)

G Sus 4th

Chord Spelling
1st (G), 4th (C), 5th (D)

G Dom 7th sus4

Chord Spelling
1st (G), 4th (C), 5th (D),
♭7th (F)

G Major 6th

Chord Spelling
1st (G), 3rd (B), 5th (D),
6th (E)

G Minor 6th

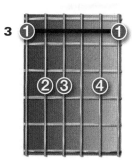

Chord Spelling
1st (G), ♭3rd (B♭), 5th (D),
6th (E)

A♭ Major

Chord Spelling
1st (A♭), 3rd (C), 5th (E♭)

A♭ Minor

Chord Spelling
1st (A♭), ♭3rd (C♭), 5th (E♭)

A♭ Major 7th

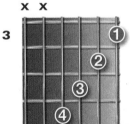

Chord Spelling
1st (A♭), 3rd (C), 5th (E♭),
7th (G)

A♭ Minor 7th

Chord Spelling
1st (A♭), ♭3rd (C♭), 5th (E♭),
♭7th (G♭)

A♭ Sus 4th

Chord Spelling
1st (A♭), 4th (D♭), 5th (E♭)

A♭ Dom 7th sus4

Chord Spelling
1st (A♭), 4th (D♭), 5th (E♭),
7th (G♭)

A♭ Major 6th

Chord Spelling
1st (A♭), 3rd (C), 5th (E♭),
6th (F)

A♭ Minor 6th

Chord Spelling
1st (A♭), ♭3rd (C♭), 5th (E♭),
6th (F)

1
2
3
4
5
6
7
8
9
10
11
12

A Major

Chord Spelling
1st (A), 3rd (C♯), 5th (E)

A Minor

Chord Spelling
1st (A), ♭3rd (C), 5th (E)

A Major 7th

Chord Spelling
1st (A), 3rd (C♯), 5th (E),
7th (G♯)

A Minor 7th

Chord Spelling
1st (A), ♭3rd (C), 5th (E),
♭7th (G)

A Sus 4th

Chord Spelling
1st (A), 4th (D), 5th (E)

A Dom 7th sus4

Chord Spelling
1st (A), 4th (D), 5th (E),
♭7th (G)

A Major 6th

Chord Spelling
1st (A), 3rd (C♯), 5th (E),
6th (F♯)

A Minor 6th

Chord Spelling
1st (A), ♭3rd (C), 5th (E),
6th (F♯)

B♭ Major

Chord Spelling
1st (B♭), 3rd (D), 5th (F)

B♭ Minor

Chord Spelling
1st (B♭), ♭3rd (D♭), 5th (F)

B♭ Major 7th

Chord Spelling
1st (B♭), 3rd (D), 5th (F),
7th (A)

B♭ Minor 7th

Chord Spelling
1st (B♭), ♭3rd (D♭), 5th (F),
♭7th (A♭)

B♭ Sus 4th

Chord Spelling
1st (B♭), 4th (E♭), 5th (F)

B♭ Dom 7th sus4

Chord Spelling
1st (B♭), 4th (E♭), 5th (F),
♭7th (A♭)

B♭ Major 6th

Chord Spelling
1st (B♭), 3rd (D), 5th (F),
6th (G)

B♭ Minor 6th

Chord Spelling
1st (B♭), ♭3rd (D♭), 5th (F),
6th (G)

325

B Major

Chord Spelling
1st (B), 3rd (D♯), 5th (F♯)

B Minor

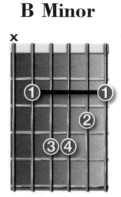

Chord Spelling
1st (B), ♭3rd (D), 5th (F♯)

B Major 7th

Chord Spelling
1st (B), 3rd (D♯), 5th (F♯),
7th (A♯)

B Minor 7th

Chord Spelling
1st (B), ♭3rd (D), 5th (F♯),
♭7th (A)

B Sus 4th

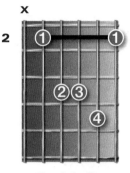

Chord Spelling
1st (B), 4th (E), 5th (F♯)

B Dom 7th sus4

Chord Spelling
1st (B), 4th (E), 5th (F♯),
♭7th (A)

B Major 6th

Chord Spelling
1st (B), 3rd (D♯), 5th (F♯),
6th (G♯)

B Minor 6th

Chord Spelling
1st (B), ♭3rd (D), 5th (F♯),
6th (G♯)

C Major

Scale pattern: C D E F G A B C

C Major Pentatonic

Scale pattern: C D E G A C

C Natural Minor

Scale pattern: C D E♭ F G A♭ B♭ C

C Minor Pentatonic

Scale pattern: C E♭ F G B♭ C

C Harmonic Minor

Scale pattern: C D E♭ F G A♭ B C

C Melodic Minor

Scale pattern: C D E♭ F G A B C

329

D♭ Major

Scale pattern: D♭ E♭ F G♭ A♭ B♭ C D♭

D♭ Major Pentatonic

Scale pattern: D♭ E♭ F A♭ B♭ D♭

C♯ Natural Minor

Scale pattern: C♯ D♯ E F♯ G♯ A B C♯

C# Minor Pentatonic

Scale pattern: C# E F# G# B C#

C# Harmonic Minor

Scale pattern: C# D# E F# G# A B# C#

C# Melodic Minor

Scale pattern: C# D# E F# G# A# B# C#

D Major

Scale pattern: D E F♯ G A B C♯ D

D Major Pentatonic

Scale pattern: D E F♯ A B D

D Natural Minor

Scale pattern: D E F G A B♭ C D

D Minor Pentatonic

Scale pattern: D F G A C D

D Harmonic Minor

Scale pattern: D E F G A B♭ C♯ D

D Melodic Minor

Scale pattern: D E F G A B C♯ D

E♭ Major

Scale pattern: E♭ F G A♭ B♭ C D E♭

E♭ Major Pentatonic

Scale pattern: E♭ F G B♭ C E♭

E♭ Natural Minor

Scale pattern: E♭ F G♭ A♭ B♭ C♭ D♭ E♭

E♭ Minor Pentatonic

Scale pattern: E♭ G♭ A♭ B♭ D♭ E♭

E♭ Harmonic Minor

Scale pattern: E♭ F G♭ A♭ B♭ C♭ D E♭

E♭ Melodic Minor

Scale pattern: E♭ F G♭ A♭ B♭ C D E♭

E Major

Scale pattern: E F♯ G♯ A B C♯ D♯ E

E Major Pentatonic

Scale pattern: E F♯ G♯ B C♯ E

E Natural Minor

Scale pattern: E F♯ G A B C D E

E Minor Pentatonic

Scale pattern: E G A B D E

E Harmonic Minor

Scale pattern: E F# G A B C D# E

E Melodic Minor

Scale pattern: E F# G A B C# D# E

F Major

Scale pattern: F G A B♭ C D E F

F Major Pentatonic

Scale pattern: F G A C D F

F Natural Minor

Scale pattern: F G A♭ B♭ C D♭ E♭ F

F Minor Pentatonic

Scale pattern: F A♭ B♭ C E♭ F

F Harmonic Minor

Scale pattern: F G A♭ B♭ C D♭ E F

F Melodic Minor

Scale pattern: F G A♭ B♭ C D E F

F♯ Major

Scale pattern: F♯ G♯ A♯ B C♯ D♯ E♯ F♯

F♯ Major Pentatonic

Scale pattern: F♯ G♯ A♯ C♯ D♯ F♯

F♯ Natural Minor

Scale pattern: F♯ G♯ A B C♯ D E F♯

340

F♯ Minor Pentatonic

Scale pattern: F♯ A B C♯ E F♯

F♯ Harmonic Minor

Scale pattern: F♯ G♯ A B C♯ D E♯ F♯

F♯ Melodic Minor

Scale pattern: F♯ G♯ A B C♯ D♯ E♯ F♯

G Major

Scale pattern: G A B C D E F♯ G

G Major Pentatonic

Scale pattern: G A B D E G

G Natural Minor

Scale pattern: G A B♭ C D E♭ F G

G Minor Pentatonic

Scale pattern: **G B♭ C D F G**

G Harmonic Minor

Scale pattern: **G A B♭ C D E♭ F♯ G**

G Melodic Minor

Scale pattern: **G A B♭ C D E F♯ G**

343

A♭ Major

Scale pattern: A♭ B♭ C D♭ E♭ F G A♭

A♭ Major Pentatonic

Scale pattern: A♭ B♭ C E♭ F A♭

G♯ Natural Minor

Scale pattern: G♯ A♯ B C♯ D♯ E F♯ G♯

G♯ Minor Pentatonic

Scale pattern: G♯ B C♯ D♯ F♯ G♯

G♯ Harmonic Minor

Scale pattern: G♯ A♯ B C♯ D♯ E F✗ G♯

G♯ Melodic Minor

Scale pattern: G♯ A♯ B C♯ D♯ E♯ F✗ G♯

345

A Major

Scale pattern: A B C♯ D E F♯ G♯ A

A Major Pentatonic

Scale pattern: A B C♯ E F♯ A

A Natural Minor

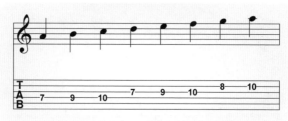

Scale pattern: A B C D E F G A

A Minor Pentatonic

Scale pattern: A C D E G A

A Harmonic Minor

Scale pattern: A B C D E F G♯ A

A Melodic Minor

Scale pattern: A B C D E F♯ G♯ A

B♭ Major

Scale pattern: B♭ C D E♭ F G A B♭

B♭ Major Pentatonic

Scale pattern: B♭ C D F G B♭

B♭ Natural Minor

Scale pattern: B♭ C D♭ E♭ F G♭ A♭ B♭

B♭ Minor Pentatonic

Scale pattern: **B♭ D♭ E♭ F A♭ B♭**

B♭ Harmonic Minor

Scale pattern: **B♭ C D♭ E♭ F G♭ A B♭**

B♭ Melodic Minor

Scale pattern: **B♭ C D♭ E♭ F G A B♭**

B Major

Scale pattern: B C♯ D♯ E F♯ G♯ A♯ B

B Major Pentatonic

Scale pattern: B C♯ D♯ F♯ G♯ B

B Natural Minor

Scale pattern: B C♯ D E F♯ G A B

B Minor Pentatonic

Scale pattern: B D E F♯ A B

B Harmonic Minor

Scale pattern: B C♯ D E F♯ G A♯ B

B Melodic Minor

Scale pattern: B C♯ D E F♯ G♯ A♯ B

351

11

Electric Guitar Care

There is more to the electric guitar than just playing. You need to know the best strings to choose and how to fit them; it is essential to know the basics of guitar care and maintenance and which tools is it useful to have to carry out simple repair jobs. We will give you some top tips on how to customize your guitar, and what to do in the event of the electrics going wrong.

Choosing Strings

Strings are the voice of your guitar. The right strings will make your guitar sound great, feel fantastic and last much longer than a cheaper set, so buy the most expensive set you can afford. Your guitar and your ears will thank you for it.

Wound and Plain

Strings are either 'wound' (rhymes with round) or 'plain'. Wound strings are two separate strings wound together. Plain strings are simply a single length of wire. Both wound and plain strings have a ball attached to one end, enabling the string to be attached to the guitar bridge. Nylon strings mostly

The 'gauge' of a string is the technical term for its diameter.

354

do not have this ball end, although some beginner's sets do have a ball, as it makes the string easier to attach.

Strings are sold in packs of six and each string has a different 'gauge' (diameter in thousandths of an inch). A 'regular gauge' set (or '10 set') of electric-guitar strings will have diameters of (from high E to low E) .010, .013, .017, .026, .036 and .046. There is a lighter-gauge '9 set', made up of strings with gauges .009, .011, .016, .024, .032 and .042. There are lighter- and heavier-gauge sets; individual strings may be mixed and matched.

What To Choose?

If you're starting out on electric guitar, choose a lighter-gauge set of nickel-steel strings and play with them for a week or so. Then try other gauges to find the one that best suits your playing style and the tone you wish to achieve.

Fitting Strings

To fit a new string, pass the ball end through the bridge of the guitar, either from the back or through the back of the bridge, depending on the model of your guitar. Tug the string firmly to seat the ball end and pass the string up to the machine heads. Turn the machine-head key until the hole in the shaft is pointing down at the string.

Wind it Through

Pass the string through the machine head leaving enough slack to enable the string to be pulled about 8 cm (3 in) from the fingerboard. Bring the loose end clockwise around the shaft and tuck it under the string as it enters the string post. Turn the key so the string is wound on to the post, trapping the loose end under the new winding. Repeat for each of the other strings. If your headstock is 'three a side', you'll need to pass the loose end clockwise around the post for the G, B and E strings to trap the end successfully.

356

Immediately after fitting, place the guitar on your knee in the playing position and place the flat of your thumb under the low E string. Push the string firmly away from the guitar. Repeat for each string. Now retune and stretch again. You should find that you can repeat this three or four times before the guitar remains roughly in tune after stretching.

When you have fitted the new strings, wipe a soft cloth dipped in three-in-one oil over the strings and saddle. This will prolong the life of your strings and also keep height adjustment screws from seizing up.

Stretching new strings once fitted helps tuning stability.

Guitar Care

Your guitar is a living, breathing instrument. The wood of your guitar is porous, with hundreds of thousands of tiny holes. These holes trap moisture, swell and contract, and can make your guitar change its mood overnight if not looked after.

Golden Rules of Care

Never keep your guitar anywhere that you would not be happy yourself. That means not storing it under the bed, hung on a wall above a radiator or put at

A glass of water left in a centrally heated room can stop guitars drying out.

the back of the garage for the winter. Seasonal change spells danger for the guitar. Your instrument can experience extreme changes in temperature just on the journey from the house to the car. Invest in a moulded case with a waterproof seal to check the ingress of moisture into the case (SKB and Hiscox have a fine selection). A packet or two of silica gel can be placed inside the case to absorb the moisture evaporating from the guitar. In winter, travel with your guitar in the car rather than the unheated boot.

Inside the house your guitar should be on a guitar stand away from radiators or sources of heat. In dry conditions place a glass of water near the guitar stand and, if you do have to leave the guitar in storage for more than a few months, do not take the strings off! Your guitar was made to be under tension and removing the strings will enable the neck to twist and warp. In short, make your guitar as comfortable as you would be yourself. But don't forget that the best thing you can do to keep your guitar in premium condition is to pick it up regularly and play it!

Keep it Clean

When cleaning your guitar, use as little domestic cleaning product (furniture spray or silicone-based polish) as possible. Use a little white automotive polishing compound to take off the grease and grime; then use clean cotton cutting cloth to bring up the original finish.

Use a tack rag (a cotton cloth moistened with light machine oil) to wipe down the bridge and other hardware. The tack rag will also do a good job on

the metal pickup covers, but watch out for metal pieces that will stick to the magnets and fur up your tone. A clean tack rag moistened

Care for the finish of your guitar by buffing immediately after each practice with a soft cloth.

with a little WD-40 is as good as any shop-bought product when used along a dirty string.

Unfinished fingerboards of ebony or rosewood can be helped with a little lemon oil or olive oil rubbed well into the grain. Finished maple fingerboards can be treated like the body of the guitar.

The plastic parts of your guitar can be treated with the same white automotive compound but may need a little silicone spray polish on a soft cloth when buffing back. Be careful with the control surfaces

that may be screen-printed 'Rhythm/ Treble' or similar. The printed words can be rubbed off if you use too much force, and can't be rubbed back into view.

Wipe the strings down after every performance or practice.

Tools

Gather the following items, and you'll be ready for your own guitar-maintenance tasks.

Get a **Philips #2** and **flat-bladed screwdriver** with a high-quality tip. Use screwdrivers with rubber grips, which won't harm a glassy finish when the tool is dropped.

You will need a full set of **'Allen'** or **hex keys** in US (inches) and European (metric) sizes. A set of **nut drivers** or **box spanners** is also useful for truss-

rod adjustments on Gibson guitars and some others.

A set of fine **modeller's files** is vital for removing burrs from bridges and nuts. **000-gauge synthetic**

A side cutter is a useful tool for cutting wires and trimming strings.

362

steel wool and **glass paper** are also useful for removing shallow scratches. A very fine **modeller's saw** is also useful for cutting nut slots.

On painted surfaces, holes can be filled with **automotive fibreglass filler** and rubbed smooth before spraying. **Liquid abrasives** are good for cutting back around shallow scratches.

A good-quality **soldering iron** with variable heat is vital for perfect solder joints on electrical components.

Side (or **wire**) **cutters** are essential for trimming excess wire and snipping untidy guitar strings from the headstock. **Needle nose pliers** are useful if you have to hold cables within a cavity. **Crocodile clips** or **locking clamps** make tricky wiring jobs easier.

Low-tack **masking tape** is essential. **High-speed glue** is useful, but doesn't stand up well to handling or moisture. Use a **high-quality epoxy** instead and smooth the excess with glass paper.

Fret Care

Frets are hardwearing and fragile at the same time. With normal use your guitar will last for years without needing a re-fret. Dented or badly worn frets can be brought back into line with a crowning file and some fine needle files and steel wool.

Replacing Frets

Draw the needle files over the fret, taking as little material off the fret as possible. When the top of the fret is as smooth you can get it, take the crowning file

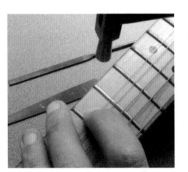

over the top of the fret to bring back the rounded shoulder of the fret. Finish with some fine steel wool.

A loose fret can cause string buzzing. Tap the loose fret into place with a small hammer or remove carefully with pliers.

Cleaning Frets

Place low-tack masking tape between the frets until you can't see the wooden fingerboard and only the crowns of each fret are exposed. Use a pad of very fine 000-grade synthetic steel wool. Wipe very gently over the tops of the frets along the length of the guitar neck. Brush off the grime and polish the sides of each fret using a soft toothbrush. Never use any metal polish, only hard cotton cutting cloth and some firm rubbing to bring the nickel silver right up.

Remove the tape, wipe the fingerboard over with lemon oil and wipe down again. After you've cleaned

the frets and neck, re-string and check the guitar's action, intonation and relief.

You can also use a proprietary string cleaner such as Fast-Fret, which conditions the fretboard and can stop the wood from drying out or warping.

Setting The Action

The 'action' of the guitar is a combination of string height, intonation and neck relief, and it refers to how the guitar feels when played.

String Height

String height on all electric guitars can be adjusted at the bridge. Most players prefer to have the strings as close as possible to the fingerboard without the buzzing or false tones that are produced when the vibrating string meets the frets or top of the pickup.

The gap between the bottom of the low E string and the top of the seventh fret should be about 0.33 mm (0.013 inches).

Depending on the model of the guitar, the individual string saddles or even the whole bridge can be adjusted to whatever height is suitable. Adjustments should always be made with the guitar tuned to concert pitch. Make small changes to the height of the bridge saddles before retuning and playing at the top of the neck close to the pickups. Listen for rattles caused by the strings meeting the frets and, if possible, listen with the guitar plugged into an amp.

Guitar Bridges

Guitar bridges trap muck and grease from your hands and if left they will rust and eventually stick. Use a small amount of penetrating oil or 'Plus Gas' on the screws and other moving parts, then set aside for a couple of hours before trying again. A stuck bridge needs more maintenance than just a simple wipe over with oil, but a can of WD-40 in the guitar case comes in handy for emergencies.

Customize Your Guitar

It needn't cost the earth to customize your guitar.
With a little patience and a few basic tools, it is
simple to make your guitar your own.

New Pickups

Pickups are simple to replace and offer the very best
return for your money. Most stock guitars aren't
fitted with the very best pickups for a number of
reasons. Replacing the stock pickups with beefed-up
'aftermarket' parts will give your guitar a better
tone. Replacement pickups are designed to slot
straight into the holes left by the other pickups. You
can often use the old screws and springs too. Stock

single-coil pickups may be 'two-
wire' pickups – hot and ground.
Replacement pickups for the
same guitar may be two- or even

By changing your pickups you can change the tone of your guitar.

five-wire pickups. The latter can simply be attached using two-wire instructions. It's not necessary to use all five conductors if you do not want to. Choose a new pickup from Seymour Duncan, DiMarzio or one of the newer manufacturers, such as Bare Knuckle.

New Hardware

After pickups, the second most popular aftermarket part is a new bridge. Replacement bridges are available for all models of guitar and are very popular because a new bridge can be easier to adjust and will probably hold the adjustment longer than a stock bridge. Fitting is easy, but take your guitar to the dealer when you choose your bridge just in case there is a difference in dimensions. Guitars from the Far East often have parts that are slightly smaller than similar parts from Europe or the USA. A worthwhile alternative to a whole new bridge is a new set of bridge saddles. Special saddles are now available that will actually help your strings to last longer (String Savers), and they are well worth the minimal expense.

Control Knobs, Scratchplates

& Other Hardware

Check out suppliers Pincotts, Stewart Macdonalds or
Allparts for groovy multi-coloured control knobs and
scratchplates (pickguards). Replacing a scratchplate
takes about an hour of your time and the results can
be truly spectacular.

A New Paint Job

Take off all the hardware, ideally remove the neck
and rub down the old finish with very fine steel wool
until the guitar is extremely smooth to the touch.

Scratchplates stop damage occurring to the guitar's body and can
also add decoration to the instrument.

Then attach the body to a piece of wood using the bolt holes in the heel, and let go with a few cans of your favourite automotive spray paint. Take a tip from the experts and always spray outside on a windless day (unless you have a very expensive custom spray booth in your house). Use short, even strokes and do anything to avoid drips or runs in the paint. Wait 12 hours between coats and at least 48 hours after the final coat before you go near it with finishing compound. Practice makes perfect, so do not use your favourite guitar. Old American, English

 or Japanese guitars are also a bad choice for a re-spray, as the best-selling prices always go to un-refinished instruments.

Bodies can be completely refinished using automotive spray paint.

Cables

The electric guitar and amplifier are usually connected by a guitar lead or cable.

Copper Cables

The 'hot'-stranded copper-wire core of the guitar cable needs to be both flexible and high quality.

Some manufacturers, such as Planet Waves, sell guitar cables with two very high-quality cores. The central cores overlap to encourage noise cancellation along the length of the cable.

Spending a bit more on good-quality cables may not seem like a priority, but given that some of the newest releases are guaranteed for life, it could be money well spent.

Jack Plugs

Jack plugs have two signal paths: the ground connection is made along the shaft of the plug, while signal connections are made through the tip. The dark band between the shaft and the tip is insulating material separating the signal from the ground. A short circuit would be created if these were to be connected, and the guitar cord would stop working.

Fixing Broken Cables

Guitar cables fail either because a jack connector has been damaged or because the wire is broken. To check a jack plug, unscrew the metal barrel. If the hot connection has come away, either solder it back on or buy a new lead. A broken wire is more difficult to detect and it's usually more efficient to buy a new cable. Guitar cables with moulded plugs cannot be repaired without replacing the jack plugs and are usually discarded after breaking.

Troubleshooting

Here are a few common problems and simple remedies.

Dull or Scratchy Volume & Tone Control

Carbon tracks inside the tone control become worn with age and use. Remove the scratchplate or rear cover and apply contact cleaner to the inside of the potentiometer through the small space in the metal can above the solder connections. Work the control backwards and forwards to ease the fluid along the track. The volume pot will have to be replaced if this procedure fails to solve the problem

Noisy Switching

Pickup selector switches fail over time as the point of contact inside the switch becomes dirty or broken. This usually results in pickups not seeming to work,

374

a big problem, but one that can easily be resolved. Spray contact cleaner (Servisol) inside the switch and move the selector to work the fluid into the contacts. If the problem doesn't go away, remove the rear cover or scratchplate and examine the switch. Check for loose or missing wiring. Finally, consider having the switch replaced with a new one.

Problems with the Jack Socket

The jack socket is a weak point on the guitar. If the instrument appears to work only when the barrel of the jack plug is pushed to one side you have a bent or corroded socket. Remove the control plate or scratchplate and gently squeeze the long spring arm

towards the centre hole. Gently rub with a little fine glass paper to remove corrosion; then test.

The jack sockets are most vulnerable to damage

Humming or Noise that Stops when the Strings of the Guitar are Touched

This problem indicates poor grounding of the guitar. Remove the rear cover or scratchplate and look for a grounding wire connecting the metal can of the volume pot to the bridge of your guitar. Replace if this connection is missing or broken on your Stratocaster or Telecaster guitar. This ground wire is missing on Les Paul-style guitars. Unfortunately, most Les Paul guitars have a hum problem because

 the electronics in these instruments are shielded with a metal 'can'. Les Paul copies don't

Copper tape can be used to deal with humming or any other noise that stops when the strings are touched.

have the can and also don't have the ground wire. Adding a ground wire between the bridge and ground will help protect your Les Paul-style guitar from noise. Electric foil or conductive paint should completely cover the walls of the cavity containing the electronics.

'Furry' Pickups

Pickups attract metal particles from strings and other metal parts of the guitar. Over time these can cause the sound from the pickup to lose definition. Use Blu-Tack to remove the metal particles by dabbing around the pickups, paying attention to the small gaps between the cover and the pole pieces.

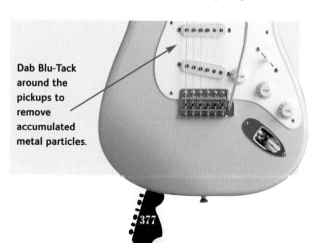

Dab Blu-Tack around the pickups to remove accumulated metal particles.

1

2

3

4

5

6

7

8

9

10

11

12

12

Resources

This section is all about helping you
become a better guitarist. There is a
useful glossary that will remind you of
key terms used in the book. We help
expand your knowledge of the guitar
and music by pointing you in the
direction of other great guitar books
and internet sites that you might find
useful. Whatever you do,
enjoy your music!

1

2

3

4

5

6

7

8

9

10

11

12

Glossary

Action The 'action' of a guitar is commonly considered to be the height of the strings from the fingerboard, which determines how much pressure you have to put on the strings in order to play them. Technically, the 'action' of the guitar is a combination of string height, intonation and neck relief.

Arpeggio An arpeggio is the sounding of the notes of a chord in succession rather than all simultaneously. These can be played individually while holding a chord down or by picking out the notes separately on the fingerboard, just as you would when playing a scale.

Barre Chord A barre chord is a chord where one of a guitarist's fretting fingers (usually the first finger) is held down across many or all of the strings in addition to other fingers holding down separate notes. Barre chords can be used in all of the 12 different keys simply by moving them up or down the fingerboard.

Bottleneck A technique in which a player moves a glass or metal bar or tube up and down the guitar neck while playing, to produce sliding pitches.

Box Shape Most guitarists usually learn scales as box-shapes, which show the finger positions for notes in a particular region of the fingerboard. The pentatonic scale, for example, can be played using five box-shapes that cover the whole guitar neck.

Dot Marker Most guitars have these markers along the neck to help players navigate the fingerboard. They are usually behind the 3rd, 5th, 7th, 9th, 12th, 15th, 17th, 19th and 21st frets of the fingerboard.

Flatpicking Flatpicking is a style where all notes, scalar and chordal, are articulated with a plectrum.

Fret Frets are metal strips placed across the radius of a guitar's fingerboard to mark out notes a semitone apart. They make it easy for a guitarist to find precise notes in scales and chords. Frets come in all shapes and sizes: some are narrow while others are wide; and some are flat at the top while others are rounded.

Glissando When a guitarist plays a glissando, he or she is sliding up or down the guitar neck in such a way that every note under the left-hand finger is articulated. This is different from a basic slide, in which the only notes that can be clearly heard are the first and last notes played by the left-hand finger.

Hammer-on A hammer-on is a technique in which you play a note behind a fret on the fingerboard and then hammer one of your other fingers down behind another fret higher up on the same string. It is one of the most common lead-guitar techniques used by blues, rock, jazz and even classical players.

Lick A lick is a small musical motif such as a phrase or riff that can be incorporated into a lead-guitar solo. All good soloists have a vocabulary of licks that they use in their lead lines.

Palm Muting You can mute a guitar's strings by placing your right hand lightly across them. This is very useful if you're playing at high volume and don't want the strings to ring out unnecessarily. It can also be used to add more colour and texture to a rhythm or solo.

Pull-off A pull-off can be seen as the reverse of a hammer-on. In this case, a note is played and then the finger playing that note is pulled off the string to sound a lower note that is either an open string or one fretted by another finger.

Riff A riff is a short series of chords or notes that can be repeated to form a catchy sequence. Some riffs are so effective that they more or less take up a whole song!

Saddle This is the place on the guitar's bridge for supporting the strings. The distance between it and the nut determines the scale length (length of vibrating open string) of a guitar.

Semitone The smallest interval between two notes on a fretted guitar is called a semitone (S). Notes on either side of a fret are separated by a semitone. An interval of two semitones is called a tone (T).

Slide This effect is produced when you play one note on the guitar and, while still holding the note down, slide up or down the guitar neck to another note. In a true slide, the only two notes you can hear clearly are the first and last notes, at the beginning and end of the slide, whereas a glissando is a sliding effect that is played in such a way that every note under the finger is articulated.

Tremelo Arm This is also known as a 'whammy bar'. It is a mechanical arm attached to the bridge of an electric guitar that can alter the pitch of the strings; as the arm is depressed, the pitch of a note played drops, and when the arm is let go, the altered pitch returns to normal.

Truss Rod This is a metal bar used for reinforcing and adjusting a steel-strung guitar's neck. It can be adjusted to keep the neck straight if the tension in it changes when different gauge strings are used.

Vibrato Vibrato is a left-hand technique (or right hand if you're left-handed) in which a played note is moved rapidly to produce a fluctuation in pitch that gives more richness to the tone. Vibrato can be applied vertically (across the neck) or horizontally (along the neck). Vibrato is used extensively in classical guitar music, and in blues, jazz and rock solos.

FLAME TREE | PUBLISHING
MUSIC PORTAL

Hear Chords and Scales
FLAMETREEMUSIC.COM

Expert Music Information
FLAMETREEPRO.COM

Sheet Music Playlists
FLAMETREEPIANO.COM

The **FLAME TREE MUSIC PORTAL** brings **chords** and **scales** you can see *and* hear, an **Expert Music search engine** on a wide range of genres, styles, artists and instruments, and free access to **playlists** for our sheet music series.

Other FLAME TREE music books include:

Guitar Chords by Jake Jackson
Piano & Keyboard Chords by Jake Jackson
Beginners Guide to Reading Music by Jake Jackson
The Jazz and Blues Encyclopedia (Editor: Howard Mandel)
Definitive Opera Encyclopedia (Founding Editor: Stanley Sadie)
Sheet Music for Piano: Scott Joplin by Alan Brown

See our full range of books at **flametreepublishing.com**